What some experts are saying about Walter Staples and this book

He's done it again! Dr. Staples has hit the major issues in personal performance head on. This book opens your eyes to the critical determinant of happiness and effectiveness in life, and shows you how to develop everything you do.

—Brian Tracy
Maximum Achievement

What a powerful book for anyone seeking to grow personally and professionally in our changing world! Walter Staples presents clearly and persuasively a solid blueprint for understanding ourselves—and for securing our success. I recommend it unreservedly.

—Nido R. Qubein
past chairman, National Speakers Association

This book has an important message—how to master the process of personal empowerment to help ourselves and others live fuller, more productive lives.

—Dr. Denis Waitley
The Psychology of Winning and
Seeds of Greatness

If you're looking for the key to success, look no farther. Dr. Staples' new book will tell you how to unlock the power within. (Personally, I'm still looking for the lock!)

—Peter McWilliams
Life 101 and
Wealth 101

If you're reading this, consider yourself lucky—you've stumbled across one of the best books ever written. Walter Staples has put so much wisdom and so many practical strategies for success into this book that it could have been three books. What a treasure chest for anyone serious about greater success and more happiness in every area of life.

—Jack Canfield
Chicken Soup for the Soul

Dr. Staples has pulled all the magic together from a myriad of sources and has blended it in his own special style into a fascinating journey into our minds, hearts and spirits. We will all be blessed and inspired by this book, as we all face the challenges described within and possess the unlimited power to overcome.

—Les Brown
Live Your Dreams

Throughout the history of man, all the great thinkers and philosophers agree that successful living is rooted in successful thinking. In a clear, easy-to-follow format, this book provides a road map to transform the person you are into the person you want to be.

—Michael Le Boeuf
Fast Forward and
How to Win Customers and Keep Them for Life

Nearly everyone knows that they have more talent and knowledge than they're using, but they're not sure what to do about it. Here's a book that provides both understanding and action steps that will make a difference!

—James W. Newman
Release Your Brakes!

IN SEARCH OF YOUR TRUE SELF

21 INCREDIBLE INSIGHTS THAT WILL REVITALIZE YOUR BODY, MIND AND SPIRIT

Walter Staples

PELICAN PUBLISHING COMPANY
GRETNA 1996

*The word "Pelican" and the depiction of a pelican are trademarks
of Pelican Publishing Company, Inc., and are registered
in the U.S. Patent and Trademark Office.*

Library of Congress Cataloging-in-Publication Data

Staples, Walter Doyle.
    In search of your true self : 21 incredible insights that will
revitalize your body, mind and spirit / Walter Staples.
       p.   cm.
    ISBN 1-56554-226-6 (hardcover : alk. paper)
    1. Self-actualization (Psychology) 2. Self-perception.
I. Title.
BF637.S4S72 1996
158'.1—dc20
                                        96-12711
                                           CIP

PERMISSIONS

The author wishes to express his appreciation to those who have granted permission to use the following material:

    The Cartoonists and Writers Syndicate, New York, N.Y. 10024 for permission to print the cartoon *World of Wit* © 1992.

    The Calgary Sun, Calgary, Canada for permission to print its cartoon © 1992 by John Lartner.

    Wilshire Book Company, North Hollywood, Calif. 91605 to quote from the works of U. S. Andersen.

    Doubleday, a division of Bantam Doubleday Dell, New York, N.Y. 10036-4094 for the quote from *Your Child's Self-Esteem: The Key to His Life* © 1970 by Dorothy C. Briggs.

    The Menninger Clinic, Topeka, Kans. 66601-0829 for the quote from *Beyond Biofeedback* © 1977 by Elmer and Alyce Green.

Manufactured in the United States of America

Published by Pelican Publishing Company, Inc.
1101 Monroe Street, Gretna, Louisiana 70053

To my mother and father

and all those who have committed their lives to helping others help themselves. Sharing knowledge and insight, facilitating the understanding and learning process of who we truly are and what each of us is capable of accomplishing in our life, is a necessary and critical task, and one that no person can afford to ignore.

The quality of life in our world is a direct function of the quality of our individual contributions. As a result of the splendid efforts of the many people involved in the human potential movement, the quality and quantity of the contributions of individual men and women are increasing, and in the process will certainly benefit all of mankind.

My thanks goes out to the following notable contributors for their many ideas and insights regarding my own spiritual growth and personal development: U. S. Andersen, Dr. Ken Blanchard, Les Brown, Jack Canfield, Deepak Chopra, M.D., Dr. Steven Covey, Dr. Wayne Dyer, Dr. Shad Helmstetter, Napoleon Hill, Maxwell Maltz, Peter McWilliams, James Newman, Dr. Norman Vincent Peale, Anthony Robbins, Dr. Robert Schuller, Dr. David Schwartz, W. Clement Stone, Brian Tracy, Dr. Denis Waitley and Zig Ziglar. It is my sincere hope that this book builds on their wise counsel, and makes its own unique contribution to the general wellness of its readers.

About the Author

Walter Staples has written four books on personal and spiritual growth and professional development. He is a certified practitioner of Neuro-Linguistic Programming (NLP).

In his career, Dr. Staples has lived in many parts of the United States, Europe and Canada. It was while living in Los Angeles that he came into contact with many of the leaders in the field of personal development including Anthony Robbins, Brian Tracy, Dr. Ken Blanchard and Jim Rohn, all of whom took an interest in his work.

His book *Think Like a Winner!* is available in bookstores throughout North America and in over 35 countries around the world. It has been translated into Japanese, French, Spanish, German, Portuguese and Afrikaans.

The endorsements for his many books read like a "Who's Who" in the field of motivation including Dr. Norman Vincent Peale, Art Linkletter, Dr. Denis Waitley, Les Brown, Dr. Laurence Peter and Dr. Robert Schuller. His books and articles have been featured in many prominent national magazines including *Entrepreneur, Reader's Digest, USAir Magazine* and *America West Airlines Magazine.*

Dr. Staples has been interviewed in over 150 radio and TV programs in the U.S. and Canada. He is one of America's most highly acclaimed authors on the subject of leadership, motivation and peak performance human behavior.

He is a respected speaker, consultant and trainer for many of America's most successful sales organizations, corporations, professional associations, and championship sports teams. For information on his availability for speaking engagements and seminars, please contact:

WALTER STAPLES INTERNATIONAL
c/o Pelican Publishing Company
PHONE (504) 368-1175 • FAX (504) 368-1195

Contents

*The longest journey
is the journey inward,
for he who has chosen his destiny
has started upon his quest
for the source of his being.*

DAG HAMMARSKJOLD
FORMER SECRETARY GENERAL
OF THE UNITED NATIONS
(1905-1961)

Preface

This book admittedly represents an ambitious undertaking. After all, psychology, which is the study of human behavior and mental thought processes, is a science and isn't something we can hope to understand in a day or two or three. At the same time, psychology is something we should not ignore all of our lives. For everything that we do—with the emphasis on *everything*—has at its root basic psychological principles.

Few of us were exposed to psychological principles during our formal education. At best, we picked up ideas here and there that seemed to make some sense, although we never quite understood why. Many were altruistic pronouncements passed down from one generation to another. Supposedly, these ideas helped others overcome some problem or difficulty at one time or another in their life, and in turn could help us.

Hence most of us are going about the business of living with a huge void in our understanding of a very critical subject: ourselves. Without some insight, some understanding of who we are and why we think and act the way we do, we necessarily struggle and stumble about, wondering if we're ever going to get it right. And because most of us think that psychology is too difficult a subject to understand, we avoid making any serious attempt.

But to avoid psychology is to be defeated by it. We need not become experts in this subject to benefit from some basic principles and concepts. And this is the modest purpose of this book—to expose you to some ideas and insights that have the potential to change your life in dramatic and powerful ways that at this moment you cannot possibly begin to imagine. But will this happen to you? I suggest it will . . . but only in proportion to your willingness to bring along a few necessary tools—an open mind, a childlike curiosity, and a burning desire to learn and stretch beyond your current level of accomplishment. So equipped, we'll now begin our fascinating journey in search of our True Self.

We are potentially all things; our personality is what we are able to realize of the infinite wealth which our divine human nature contains hidden in its depth.

WILLIAM RALPH INGE
ENGLISH THEOLOGIAN AND AUTHOR
(1860-1954)

The Renaissance Program™

We are born unarmed. Our mind is our only weapon.
—Ayn Rand

Experience this odyssey into self-awareness and self-mastery, and begin to understand the inner workings of your mind. Discover how to become free, and grow in the image of your True Self.

In this, the RENAISSANCE PROGRAM, you'll discover a myriad of fascinating new ideas and concepts relating to personal and spiritual growth and professional development. In fact, many of these ideas don't exist in the current literature because they are original and unique to Dr. Staples. You'll also acquire a whole new vocabulary and learn a variety of new techniques and strategies as you begin to see how much power you actually have over your mind and body, and hence over every aspect of your life.

We are rapidly approaching the 21st century. The world today is characterized by rapid change, accelerating technological developments and unprecedented international competition. This necessarily requires more of each individual in the workforce and in all aspects of life—a greater capacity for innovation and creativity, self-development, and personal responsibility. Hence the need for empowerment—specifically, for a PROVEN process for personal empowerment.

This book focuses on over 21 incredible insights that are your key to a whole new reality, to a whole new life. They include—the Personal Empowerment Process; the True Self; the Artificial Self; the Universal Achievement Process; the Law of Creation; the Five Ultimate Questions; the Staples Principle; the Mirroring Effect; the Sensory Stimulus Trap; the A-C-E technique; the Three Pillars of the Self; the Natural Success Formula; the Comfort Zone Complex; the Quantum Leap concept; the Fail-Proof Formula for Success; the Primary Life Purpose exercise; the "push-pull" imaging technique; the Five Cups of Life; the Five Great Wonders of the Mind; the Contribution Matrix Chart; the I.C.A.N. principle™; the Great Wheel of Life; the HRR factor; and the ULTIMATE INSIGHT.

*How is it possible that a being
with such sensitive jewels as the eyes,
such enchanted musical instruments as
the ears, and such a fabulous arabesque
of nerves as the brain can experience itself
as anything less than a god?*

ALAN WATTS
AMERICAN PHILOSOPHER AND AUTHOR
OF THE SPIRIT OF ZEN
(1915-1973)

This is not just another self-help program that simply treats the symptoms and ignores the causes of personality deficiencies and human failing. It is a total RE-creation program—RE-creation in the image of who you really are—in the image of your True Self!

> To exist is to change; to change is to grow;
> to grow is to RE-create yourself endlessly.

In all aspects of life—physical, mental, spiritual, family, career and financial—the process of personal empowerment is the primary determinant, the deciding factor that dictates whether you succeed or fail. **When you become master of your inner world, you become master of your outer world.** It is the thoughts you think that are the dominant force in your existence.

At the end of each chapter, you'll find a "success story" that illustrates in detail the amazing power of a positive self-image. Each describes in a convincing and dramatic way how others in many different walks of life have had the courage and conviction to dream big dreams, and turned them into reality, often in the face of great adversity. And so can you! For the resources you need to turn your life around today—regardless of your present circumstances—**are already within you!** They are simply hidden, lying dormant, waiting to be utilized. By tapping into these vast resources, you can rise to any height, and find peace, happiness and unlimited power within you. But first you must purposely go about developing a major new asset: **a greater sense of self.**

Each of these stories is testimony to this incredible yet indisputable fact: you have been born RICH! You possess an abundance of unique and varied gifts, an immense treasure that lies buried deep inside you. Knowing this, you need only **test your outer limits** to achieve the greatness you so rightfully deserve.

The purpose of this book is to help you *unlock the magic in your mind to get the results in life you really want*. To this end, you must **think B-I-G** in all you say and do. For you cannot succeed at anything unless you are passionately interested in it and absolutely certain of achieving it. Your challenge, then, is simple and straightforward: you must find a way to set yourself on fire!

We have been blessed with the power of choice
—we can be, do and have what we want.

WALTER STAPLES

is one of America's leading authorities on human potential and personal empowerment. Thousands of people have read his books and attended his seminars around the world. His philosophy and teachings have had a dramatic and profound impact on those willing to question their fixed beliefs and explore the nature of their true selves. In this classic work, Dr. Staples shares his greatest insights and inspirational ideas with us in a unique and convincing way. **The result is nothing short of LIFE-CHANGING!**

The simplest truths are always the most powerful, if only they are understood, accepted and internalized. What is the simple truth, then, that Dr. Staples proclaims to the world—to those in all walks of life who want to **be** more and to **achieve more?** It is this:

It matters not where we were born, who our parents were, what our level of education is, what language we speak, what skills we have developed, or what successes or failures we have had. It matters only WHO WE THINK WE ARE. For if we change who we *think* we are . . .

WE CHANGE WHO WE ARE!

IN SEARCH OF YOUR TRUE SELF

*Whatever understanding we have
of ourself, this is what we become.
We can become anything we want,
because the world exists
through the power of beliefs.
There is nothing fixed or limiting
about a human being.
All the power of the universe is inside us.
Simply put, we are who we think we are,
and this we have the power to change
at any moment.*

WALTER STAPLES
MY SIGNATURE STATEMENT

CHAPTER 1

We Are Responsible for Our Life

The price of greatness is responsibility.
—Winston Churchill

The Creation of Hidden Prompters

Somewhere, in some city, a miracle is happening at this very instant: a child is being born. This child is pure spirit, pure potential cast into a human mould as a manifestation of infinite intelligence. Immediately, however, the child is impacted by a myriad of external stimuli—sights, sounds, smells and sensations—found in its new environment. And in the process, its subconscious memory is being formed, its knowledge of itself is being forged, its sense of self is being shaped.

There is something both very wonderful and very sad in this process. Wonderful because the infant is free to think its own thoughts, to explore its own potential, to decide its own future. Sad because its knowledge of its True Self is being thwarted by the mere fact of it being alive—by its experiences in an often harsh and cruel physical world. A fortunate few find happiness and fulfillment from this process, whereas a great many find only disappointment and despair. Yet there can be no other path to self-awareness, no other path to self-direction, no other path to self-actualization.

This gives us some idea of the immense challenge we all face. In our formative years, we are forced to accept messages from a chaotic and confusing world that begin to define who we are. Whether it's exposure to poverty, violence or under-achievement in school—there can be hundreds, often thousands, of negative experiences—all have their impact. From these effects we cannot hide, for there is no place to hide. And at a young age, we're not able to make informed judgments about either the validity of these messages or their relevance.

*My religion consists
of a humble admiration
of the illimitable superior spirit
who reveals Himself in the slight details
we are able to perceive
with our frail and feeble mind.*

ALBERT EINSTEIN
GERMAN-BORN PHYSICIST
(1879-1955)

These first impressions are stored in memory as childhood re-membrances, and are soon forgotten by our Conscious Mind. But they necessarily have a lasting and powerful impact, since they reappear later in life as hidden prompters. As we were growing up, most of us were not even aware that we were being influenced in an important way by all the things around us. But let there be no doubt that it has happened. And the vast majority of us spend the rest of our lives trying to undo all the damage.

The Power Within

It should be no surprise, then, that few of us see ourselves as a positive force in a negative world. Yet we're all able to make this choice if we develop the insight, the courage and the determination to travel down this path, this road less traveled, knowing we owe it to ourselves and others to make a contribution that is consistent with who we really are, and with our natural talents and abilities.

I like this quotation by Oliver Wendell Holmes: "What lies behind us and what lies before us are tiny matters compared to what lies WITHIN us." This is an insightful comment. Few of us have any idea of the immense power of our mind, that marvellous mechanism that defines for us who we are and what kind of world we live in. Seldom do we use our mind effectively to get what we want. More often than not, we use it to get exactly the opposite—what we don't want!

The largest part of our mind operates below the level of our consciousness, and is known as our Subconscious Mind. This is our true power source, for this mind is an integral part of yet a greater mind still, which we shall call Universal Mind. Universal Mind is of such power, strength and scope that we can only guess at its totality. It is an energy, an intelligence that has been given many names throughout history —the Power, the Source, the Light, the Almighty—and is regarded as eternal, infinite, all-powerful and all-knowing. All of the great monotheistic religions in the world refer to this entity as God. The particular name we give this entity is not as important as knowing it exists, and that we can use its immense powers to achieve greater understanding of ourselves and the world we live in.

*To see a world in a grain of sand
and heaven in a wild flower,
to hold infinity
in the palm of your hand,
and eternity in an hour.*

WILLIAM BLAKE
ENGLISH POET AND ENGRAVER
(1757-1827)

This vaster, invisible mind is not a person. It is not a giant-sized old man with a white beard and robe who lives somewhere up in the sky and looks down benignly on all of creation. Rather it is a living spirit, not separate from man, but an integral part of man. It is the very consciousness that dwells in you and in me—in all things and in all creatures. It has no one form, yet it is all form as it reveals to us through its many works and our own.

That a greater intelligence or higher power exists, there can be no doubt. All of the great religions in the world attest to it. Man prides himself on his many accomplishments, from towering skyscrapers to supersonic aircraft to super-computers. But a human being has never created from nothing even a grain of sand, a blade of grass or the leaf of a tree! Yet all these things exist. A power much greater than we mere humans created them. Or a thought. A human being has never "created" a thought. We have them but we don't make them.

As a life form at the current stage of our development, we have many limitations. We're all prone to weakness and anger, to idleness and self-doubt. But by knowing how to tap into this greater intelligence, this omnipotent force, our limitations vanish before our very eyes. Our minds are the most powerful creative instrument in the universe. Universal Mind spans all time and space, transforms thought into form, and contains all knowledge and all wisdom that has ever been or ever will be.

We have the same powers as our Maker, the same abilities to ponder, reflect, imagine and create. By accessing this higher power, we can discover who we really are and what our purpose is here on earth. In the process, we can find meaning, direction, fulfillment and happiness in our life.

So let's proceed on this basis: the human mind has no limits, it has no boundaries but we need to push ourselves, to stretch ourselves if we're ever to discover who we really are and what we're really made of—if we're ever to unlock the power that lies within!

PERCEPTUAL TRANSFORMATION:
Seeing life the way it can be,
not the way
it now appears.

WALTER STAPLES

The Power of the Mind

Consider the incredible power inherent in the human mind:

the power of thought	the power of desire
the power of perception	the power of belief
the power of optimism	the power of choice
the power of imagination	the power of focus
the power of decision	the power of giving
the power of persistence	the power of learning
the power of purpose	the power of love

These are some of the most empowering mental assets we can hope to harness and utilize, and they represent the essential building blocks of a dynamic and fulfilling life. And we can access all of these powers. In fact, we already have the ultimate power—the power to be whoever we want to be and do whatever we want to do. "To be what we are and to become what we are capable of being," wrote Robert Louis Stevenson, "is the only end of life." We know our natural talents and abilities are already there, hidden just beneath the surface. We all have far more potential for high achievement than we can now possibly imagine.

This program is designed to help you look deeper within yourself to discover more of these hidden resources. Once you begin to appreciate the tremendous potential you possess and your virtually unlimited capacity for accomplishment, you'll begin to see the many possibilities that are within your reach. This will usher in a dramatic new phase in your life, and help you experience what can only be called a "perceptual transformation"—of who you are and what you can accomplish during your life-time.

Remember: you were forced out of the comfort zone of the womb by Nature, but you must break out of the comfort zone you have created in your life . . . all by YOURSELF!

There are three main challenges that face any motivational speaker or author. The first is to master the subject matter you specialize in. The second is to apply the concepts and ideas in your own life. The third is to teach them to others in such a way that they are relevant, understood and have an impact. After 25 years of study and

Take a chance!
All life is a chance.
The man who goes furthest
is generally the one
who is willing to do and dare.

DALE CARNEGIE
AUTHOR OF *HOW TO WIN FRIENDS*
AND INFLUENCE PEOPLE
(1888-1955)

application, I'll be trying my very best to have an impact on you with this material, knowing that it is relevant because we all want to and we all can perform at a higher level, if only we are given some ideas on—HOW TO DO IT!

I suggest you face the same three challenges as well: to master the subject matter, apply the concepts, and teach them to others. In fact we teach others every day of our life by the personal example we set, and by the way we present ourselves and treat others.

Our Strength Lies Within Us

Consider this cartoon. The scene is in the Himalayas. The majestic mountains dominate the skyline. At the base of these mountains, two men dressed in simple robes are sitting side-by-side, arms and legs crossed, on small prayer blankets spread out on the ground. The wise man on the left appears calm and serene, at peace with himself. His eyes are closed, his head slightly bowed, and he has a gentle and knowing smile on his face. The man on the right is looking over at his colleague, and with a frown on his face and a hurt in his eyes, asks pointedly, "Do you KNOW something I don't know?"

I have found
power
in the mysteries
of thought.

EURIPIDES
GREEK TRAGIC DRAMATIST
(5TH CENTURY B.C.)

GERBERG
USA

"Do you know something I don't know?"

Mind is the great lever
of all things;
human thought is the process
by which human ends
are ultimately answered.

DANIEL WEBSTER
AMERICAN STATESMAN AND ORATOR
(1782-1852)

I can think of three things, three incredible facts, that the wise man with the knowing smile knows that his colleague, indeed most people in the world, do not:

1. Life is a series of thoughts.
2. We become what we think about.
3. We can choose what we think about.

I'll be talking more about each of these points later in the program, for they are integral to a clear understanding of how we can access the incredible power of our mind.

It's interesting to consider that these two men probably were born in the same country, speak the same language, had the same basic education and religious training, were brought up in similar physical environments . . . yet only one is able to find inner peace and contentment by simply focusing on his own thoughts. He finds strength and meaning WITHIN himself. All the while the other person goes through life in desperate search of these same things.

We know Eastern cultures historically have been more introspective, and less worldly and materialistic in their approach to life than have Western cultures.

The Universal Achievement Process

In this program, we'll be discussing what I call the Universal Achievement Process, an important topic since our sense of self comes directly from who we think we are and what we can accomplish in this world. The achievement process is indeed universal, since it applies to both our personal and professional life, to everything we attempt to do. It is the framework we use to live, to work, to dream . . . to realize our full potential.

Here are the seven main elements of the Universal Achievement Process that must be considered when pursuing a goal of any consequence:

1. Desire.

Questions: Where does it come from? How can we have it? How can we dramatically increase it?

*Fall
seven times,
stand up
eight.*

JAPANESE PROVERB

2. Clear, focused goals.

Question: What do we really want in the six key areas of our life—physical, mental, spiritual, family, career, and financial?

3. Unquestionable belief in both ourselves and our goals.

Question: How can we develop and maintain unquestionable belief in ourselves and in our goals?

4. A plan to implement our goals.

Question: What are the main elements of a successful plan?

5. Taking consistent action in the direction of our goals.

Question: How can we overcome the three biggest barriers to lasting success: doubt, fear and procrastination?

6. Assessing our results, and changing our approach.

Questions: What are we doing right? What are we doing wrong? What do we need to change in order to get back on track?

7. Keep on taking action, all the while focusing on the desired outcome.

Question: How can we keep on taking action in the face of setbacks and frustrations, and when the goal is still far from being realized?

All these steps are critical to anyone who wants to accomplish anything of any real significance as an individual. In fact, they are hallmarks of all successful people. People who don't have goals and who don't take action, don't get any results. Action—focused, consistent action—is the precursor of all great accomplishment. In fact, we learn by **doing,** we do by **doing,** and we self-actualize by **doing!**

To the dull mind,
all nature is leaden.
To the illuminated mind,
the whole world burns
and sparkles with light.

RALPH WALDO EMERSON
AMERICAN ESSAYIST,
PHILOSOPHER AND POET
(1803-1882)

The same steps have implications as well for leaders, for those responsible for achieving results by working with and through other people—for example, a manager, a teacher, a coach, a pastor, a politician or a parent. Leaders are in the business of empowering others, and need to develop key communications skills that relate to motivating, goal-setting, directing, team-building, planning, delegating, monitoring, training, appraising, counseling and rewarding.

Our focus in this book will be on what we can do as individuals to empower ourselves, to make something of ourselves, and be free from the whims of other people and events in our life. **If we accept that we are in charge, we must find a way to be in control.** Quite obviously, if we don't know how to empower ourselves, it's unlikely we're able to empower others. It's impossible to be an effective leader if we don't know who we are, where we're going, and how we're going to get there.

As we proceed, you'll begin to find the answers to the many questions just posed along with the seven main elements of the Universal Achievement Process. As these answers become clear to you, experiment with them and begin to apply them in a purposeful way in your daily life.

Who Motivates Whom?

A simple exercise. Assume that I was addressing a large, live audience today instead of talking to you from the pages of this book. And that I asked all the people in the room to stand up and introduce themselves to others around them, and share their name and what they did for a living. Having done this, I would proceed to discuss what just happened in light of what's called the "pleasure-pain" principle. This principle says that people in life are naturally attracted toward perceived pleasurable things and repelled away from perceived painful things. Having asked everyone in the room to perform this task, I would have noted that everyone carried it out. It would appear that everybody was fairly comfortable with the exercise, finding perhaps no great pleasure in it but also no great pain.

*Most individuals haven't given
a half-hour's uninterrupted thought
to deciding or even thinking about
what they will be or what they will do,
yet these are two of the most
significant choices we each have.*

JAMES R. BALL
FROM *SOAR . . . IF YOU DARE*

Now ask yourself this question. In this exercise, did I "motivate" anyone in the room to do anything? In a very real sense, I did not. Because I can't motivate anyone to do anything—without his or her consent. I can, of course, plant a seed, an idea in people's minds to do something. **But I can't "cause" them to do it.** People make such a decision all by themselves based on their evaluation of it in light of their perception of ensuing pleasure or pain.

It's the same with the advice in this book. I can cite all kinds of benefits you'll receive if you're willing to work on yourself and on certain concepts. But I can't "make" you do anything. I can recommend, suggest, even cajole. But in the end, any decision TO ACT . . . is totally yours.

So let there be no doubt where the final responsibility lies if you hope to benefit in a significant way from this material. It lies with YOU, and YOU alone. Any desire to change, to grow, to achieve anything of any real significance must come from WITHIN YOU. And once you understand and accept this fact, you'll come to realize that you wouldn't want it any other way!

As we'll see, accepting responsibility is not a passive act. It translates into taking the initiative and "learning and earning" your way—keeping focused and following through no matter what the odds are against you. In other words, you must always **pay the price** that has to be paid in order to get the results you earnestly want. Then, and only then, you'll be truly on your way. For as James Allen, author of the marvelous little book *As a Man Thinketh,* has correctly noted, "You cannot travel within and stand still without."

*The way you activate
the seeds of your creation
is by making choices
about the results you want to create.
When you make a choice,
you mobilize vast human energies
and resources
which otherwise go untapped.
All too often people fail
to focus their choices upon results
and therefore their choices
are ineffective.
If you limit your choices
only to what seems
possible or reasonable,
you disconnect yourself from what
you truly want,
and all that is left
is a compromise.*

ROBERT FRITZ
MOTIVATIONAL SPEAKER

YOU HAVE TO SET YOURSELF ON F-I-R-E!

RAYMOND HUNG

In 1949, Raymond Hung fled to Hong Kong with his parents to escape the Communist takeover in China. He wanted to learn more about free enterprise and start his own company, so he left Hong Kong in 1968 to attend the University of Illinois. He returned to Hong Kong in 1976 with an MBA in hand, eager to get started.

Raymond founded Applied Electronics Limited, which soon became a multi-million-dollar supplier of electronic components to major electronic firms. But he wasn't satisfied. He wanted to own a company that was a household name and employ thousands of people who shared his vision. He decided to enter the consumer products business and adopt the powerful marketing techniques of network marketing to achieve his goal.

In 1991, Raymond founded Quorum International Inc., based in Phoenix, Arizona, a firm that specializes in personal alarm and other state-of-the-art home and automobile security products. With crime on the rise, he reasoned, people increasingly needed to protect themselves and their property, and he wanted to be a major force in this industry.

Today, Raymond's company is growing in leaps and bounds, with sales of about $250 million per year. What does the future hold for his company? New products, like voice-activated devices. And new markets . . . like China, from which he fled over 40 years ago.

You make a difference by giving something of yourself for the betterment of others. Raymond Hung has made a difference. He dared to dream big dreams, and in the process, he set himself on fire!

*Every education
is a kind of
inward journey.*

VACLAV HAVEL
POET AND PRESIDENT
OF THE CZECH REPUBLIC

CHAPTER 2

Our Thoughts
Are Our Choice

To be conscious that we are perceiving or thinking
is to be conscious of our own existence.
—Aristotle

The Conscious and Subconscious Mind

A request. Take your left hand and hold it in your right hand. Easy
enough, right? Now try to hold your right hand in your right hand.
Not as easy, is it?

What's the point? The point is this: understanding all human behavior begins with understanding the mind. Why is this so difficult a
task? Because we have to use our mind to understand our mind . . .
which is very much like trying to hold our right hand in our right
hand. It is necessarily a difficult and inaccurate process. Nevertheless,
we have no choice but to try.

So what ideas or concepts will work for you? You can't hope to
know until you become a student of the subject and begin to experiment with various concepts. You will never know it all. But of course
you don't have to in order to bring about significant change and improvement in your life.

Many of us are not aware of the many successes we have already
had in life, especially those that take place at the subconscious level.
For example, we all won a major race just to get here—we all won
the sperm race! We beat out 50 million other cells to get fertilized.
Then, after birth, we all grew and matured according to some miraculous blueprint, the genetic code that's unique to each of us. As well,
we all have an incredible immune system at work inside us that keeps
us healthy and energetic day after day. Can you imagine the hundreds of diseases we fend off each year—and we don't even know it's
happening?

The ancestor
of every action
is a thought.

RALPH WALDO EMERSON
AMERICAN ESSAYIST,
PHILOSOPHER AND POET
(1803-1882)

From these examples, we see how we have been programmed by our Creator to be successful at many things at the subconscious level. Here are some other examples that illustrate the immense power of the Subconscious Mind.

Every 24 hours, WITHOUT ANY EFFORT ON OUR PART, our Subconscious Mind performs some rather incredible feats. It

- causes us to breathe 23,000 times, inhaling and exhaling 438 cubic feet of air;
- causes our heart to beat 100,000 times, or about two and a half billion times in 70 years;
- causes our heart to pump 4,300 gallons of blood, enough to fill 13 million barrels in a life-time; and
- causes our blood to make 1,450 complete circuits through 600,000 miles of capillaries.

We need to keep these statistics in mind as we begin to explore the power of our built-in success system and the extent of our full potential. And consider this: if we can do all these things by not even thinking about them, imagine what we can do if we start engaging in some real, serious THINKING!

What we need to know now is how to be more successful at the conscious level, that part of our thinking that we're aware of and for which we—and not our Creator—are totally responsible. As we'll be demonstrating, it's our Conscious Mind that controls our Subconscious. The Conscious Mind is the master practitioner that controls the obedient servant, that plants the seeds in the Subconscious Mind that then begin to blossom and grow. Understanding this, *how to program ourselves at the conscious level to be more successful,* is the master key to unlocking our full potential.

The rewards we receive in life come as a result of our performance, not our potential. This program puts our current performance in relation to our full potential into clearer focus for rational assessment. It puts these two factors into better perspective in light of information not made available to us before.

*They can
because they think
they can.*

VIRGIL
ROMAN POET
(70-19 B.C.)

Where to Begin

A brief explanation of what I'll be talking about. Often it's harder to know where to begin than where to end. Since everything is cause and effect anyway, we can trace backward—from the end we are striving for to the beginning. The relationship goes something like this:

1. successful results, come from
2. persistent, focused effort, comes from
3. clear, meaningful goals, come from
4. positive feelings about self (representing high self-esteem), come from
5. a positive self-image, comes from
6. strong core beliefs, come from
7. individual thoughts and experiences.

So we see it's our **individual thoughts and experiences** that determine our core beliefs, that determine our self-image, that determines our level of self-esteem, that determines everything else including the results we achieve.

In other words, we first have to believe in ourselves before we can expect to be successful at anything. *BELIEVE IN OURSELVES*—this is what every self-help book that's ever been written tries to do for the reader. Have you ever thought about:

• How many people believe in themselves . . . 100 percent?
• How many people believe in what they are doing . . . 100 percent?
• How many people . . . have a dream? How many people are actually following their dream, and seeing it materialize and being manifested in their life?

(continued on page 47)

𝕿HE ACHIEVEMENT CONTINUUM

We go from DENIAL . . . to DOUBT . . .
to sheer DETERMINATION

1. *HEY! No way I can!*
2. *I can't!*
3. *Can I?*
4. *Perhaps I can. . . .*
5. *I think I can.*
6. *I know I can.*
7. *I CAN!*
8. *WOW! I can move mountains!*

(Please step aside . . . I'm on FIRE!)

WALTER STAPLES
FROM THE "SET YOURSELF ON FIRE"™
GOALS SEMINAR

THE MASTER SUCCESS FORMULA

KEY QUESTIONS

A. What is CAUSE . . . and what is EFFECT?

B. What must I work on to jump-start the process?
   (work on the cause! not the effect)

C. How can I measure my progress?
   (where are you on the list below?)

Everything begins with . . .

      1. our thoughts and experiences,

that lead to

      2. our sense of self (who am I?),

that leads to

      3. our sense of self-worth (how much do I like/
      value/esteem myself?),

that leads to

      4. desire and energy,

that lead to

      5. our willingness to "learn" and "earn,"

that leads to

      6. our ability to take action,

that leads to

      7. getting some results,

that lead to

      8. excitement and fulfillment,

that lead . . .

RIGHT BACK TO #1—more positive thoughts and experiences, that lead to a greater sense of self, higher self-worth, more desire and interest . . . and the whole process repeats itself over and over again!

My mother always praised me
and made me feel good,
built my self-esteem.
All kids need this but most don't get it.
The ones that do, watch out.

PETER POCKLINGTON
ENTREPRENEUR AND OWNER
OF THE EDMONTON OILERS HOCKEY TEAM

The answer: very few indeed. This goes a long way to explain why so few people are actually excited about who they are and what they're doing. And research supports this contention.

The Public Agenda Foundation recently conducted a major survey of the American workforce, and came up with these key findings:

- less than 25 percent of jobholders say they are currently working at their full potential;
- 50 percent say they put only enough effort into their job to keep it;
- fully 75 percent say they could be significantly more effective than they presently are;
- almost 60 percent of American workers believe they do not work as hard as they used to.

Something is drastically wrong, and ideas on how to deal with the problem are few and far between. It's clear that over three- quarters of workers in America are bored, under-utilized and ineffective— they feel UNEMPOWERED—and have no idea how to help themselves or change the situation. Could the solution lie in first helping such people change their perception of themselves—who they think they are and what they're capable of doing, then giving them the necessary opportunities to prove their competence?

The Hardest Sell in the World

Have you ever given serious thought to what is the hardest "sell" in the world? You may think it's selling life insurance, used cars or magazine subscriptions door-to-door. But you would be wrong. The hardest sell in the world is

YOU selling YOU on YOURSELF!

Henry Ford once wrote, "Whether you believe you can do a thing or not, you are right." How many times have you done something successfully that you thought you couldn't? Probably not very often.

*No one
can give faith, unless he has faith;
the persuaded
persuade.*

MATTHEW ARNOLD
ENGLISH AUTHOR AND CRITIC
(1822-1888)

Why would you even try if you honestly believed you were certain to fail? How many times have you done something successfully that you thought you could? Probably very often. Why wouldn't you go for it if you honestly believed you would succeed?

The following anonymous poem titled *YOU CAN IF YOU THINK YOU CAN* expands on this important concept:

> If you think you are beaten, you are,
>> If you think you dare not, you don't.
> If you want to win but think you can't,
>> It's almost certain you won't.
>
> If you think you'll lose, you're lost,
>> For out in the world we find,
> Success begins with a person's will—
>> It's all in the state of mind.
>
> If you think you are outclassed, you are,
>> You've got to think high to rise.
> You've got to be sure of yourself before
>> You can ever win a prize.
>
> Life's battles don't always go
>> To the stronger or faster man,
> But sooner or later the one who wins,
>> Is the one *WHO THINKS HE CAN!*

So this is how the mind works—we act on the beliefs we have by bringing our inner visions into reality, whether these beliefs are true or false, positive or negative, desirable or undesirable. The following sentence describes what I believe to be the most important of all the mental laws, what I call the **Law of Creation.** It can be stated as a simple formula:

THOUGHT plus FAITH creates FORM.

In other words, we always manifest in our experience that which we are convinced of. It is through our beliefs and convictions that our thoughts are transformed into physical "things." Anything is possible for those who first conceive the image of what they desire in

𝕯eep within man
dwells those slumbering powers;
powers that would astonish him,
that he never dreamed of possessing;
forces that would revolutionize his life
if aroused and put
into action.

ORISON SWETT MARDEN
AUTHOR OF THE CLASSIC
HE CAN WHO THINKS HE CAN
(1850-1924)

their mind with great emotional intensity and firmly believe in its attainment. "If thou canst believe, all things are possible to him that believeth," we are told in the Bible. Here is a prime example.

Recall the story of the four-minute mile. For thousands of years, no one believed it was possible for a human being to run the mile in less than four minutes. But on May 6, 1954, Roger Bannister proved the impossible was possible. How did he do it? First he DECIDED it was possible to do it, and that HE would do it. He began by constantly imagining the event taking place successfully over and over again in his mind. He "saw" himself breaking through the four-minute barrier literally hundreds and hundreds of times, creating clear, convincing depictions of himself accomplishing his goal with so much emotional intensity that his subconscious and nervous system were programmed to carry it out.

His success of course prompted others to change their own belief system. Within the next 18 months, 24 other runners proceeded to break the four-minute mile. In the following decade, several hundred others accomplished the same feat. And today, ALL THE RUNNERS in such a race consistently break the four-minute mark. The barrier proved to be mental, not physical. This is a prime example of how thought plus faith creates form. Knowing now where we must begin, with our individual thoughts and experiences, let's begin here.

We Are Our Thoughts

Let's explore the concept: we are our thoughts, our thoughts are us. I was asked recently in an interview what was the most incredible thing I had learned in my life. I replied, **"It's the fact we become what we consciously think about the most—and that we can control this process by choosing the thoughts we allow our mind to entertain."** We all move in the direction of our current dominant thoughts, how we see ourselves in relation to the world we live in. To demonstrate, ask yourself—what do successful people think about most of the time? Well, successful people think about opportunities,

The highest possible stage in moral culture is when we recognize that we ought to control our thoughts.

CHARLES DARWIN
ENGLISH NATURALIST
(1809-1882)

affluence, challenge and change. They think about success! And what do unsuccessful people think about most of the time? They think about problems, poverty, set-backs, lack and limitation. They think about failure. And true to form, what each group thinks about . . . eventually comes about!

Several people have come upon this insightful discovery throughout history. For example, Plato, who died in 347 B.C. at the age of 80, said, "We become what we contemplate." In Proverbs 23:7 it says, "As a man thinketh in his heart, so is he." And the late Earl Nightingale in his classic recording, The Strangest Secret, states, "We become what we think about."

For if I know what you're thinking about, I know who you are and where you're going. It's our thoughts that determine who we are. We all create our tomorrow based on what we're thinking today. So simply by changing our thoughts, we can change who we are, and hence every aspect of our life.

Conscious Thought Control

Man has always strived to gain control over what he thinks about, his innermost thoughts and feelings. We all want to know how to run our brain more effectively in order to get more of what we want. We're often told we're in charge, that we are responsible for all our decisions and actions—in fact for our life—but we're seldom told how to exercise this responsibility. And this is what this program represents—a software program for the human system, an operator's manual for the brain.

It's tragic to note how so many people today are turned off with life. Increasingly, people are turning to recreational drugs and alcohol to get "turned on," using artificial means to reach a mental high. North Americans are responsible for 50 percent of the world's consumption of cocaine annually. But there is a fascinating alternative we can use to achieve the same ends, and even more—**and that is to get high on thoughts we choose to think for ourselves!** We can enter a whole new world of our own making by using our incredible imagination and persistent, focused effort.

*It is only when you
exercise your right to choose
that you can
exercise your right to change.*

SHAD HELMSTETTER
AUTHOR OF *CHOICES*

The world is full of problems, disasters and acts of human failing. In fact, the news media—newspapers, television and magazines— make sure we know all about them in every detail. Writers for these organizations seem to think that this is their job. We shouldn't be surprised, then, to find that most of us are haunted by negative thoughts for most of our lives.

The problem this creates is enormous and is devastating in its effect. People consumed by negative thoughts can't see beyond them. They play it safe. They don't try new things. This thing called "success" is foreign to their thinking. They can't imagine good things happening to them. And with this as their mind-set, of course good things don't. The result at best is frustration; at worst, it's depression and a deep sense of despair.

The process to end this vicious downward cycle begins by allowing more positive thoughts to dominate our daily routine. This doesn't mean we have to eliminate all negative thoughts from our life. It does mean we have to exercise more control if we want to change. You see, we're not responsible for every thought that enters our mind—**but we are responsible for every thought we allow to stay there!**

We Can Choose Our Thoughts

A prime example is writing. A writer decides on a certain topic or theme she wishes to explore. She proceeds to allow a wide range of thoughts and ideas to enter her consciousness for assessment. Some seem to come in by invitation. In fact, they all come in by themselves, and thankfully one at a time. Those thoughts she likes, she writes down; those she doesn't, she discards. She then goes about arranging all the ones that remain into something that is consistent with her initial approach. Much rearranging and many rewrites are often required to achieve all the nuances and subtleties desired. A writer could well have chosen 100,000 words to complete a book of 250 pages. And probably rejected at least a million others in the process. Whatever the result, the writer is responsible for the words and ideas she has ultimately selected, for what she has allowed "to stay there."

𝕿HOUGHTS:
Select only those that
suit your greater purpose
and let all others pass by.

WALTER STAPLES

To think, then, is not just to HAVE thoughts; to think is to SE-LECT thoughts from a wide range available to us that are consistent with a particular purpose.

It is in realizing we can EXERCISE CONTROL over the thoughts we have that is most important. And this is the critical first step in the Personal Empowerment Process that gives us some alternative to the destructive habitual thinking most of us practice in our daily lives.

Take the simple example of who or what determines the kind of day you're going to have. Now some people get up in the morning HOPING things will happen in just the right way such that they'll have a good day. They hope that the sun will be shining, that people will be nice to them, and that lady luck will be on their side. In the process, they surrender control of their well-being to forces over which they have no influence. And this is how they live each day of their life.

Other people DECIDE when they get up in the morning what kind of day they're going to have. They make a choice, in fact a decision that they're going to have a meaningful and productive day, no matter what. It doesn't matter what the weather is like, whether people are nice to them, or how lady luck plays her cards. They know what kind of day they want, and they simply go about getting it. They live with the belief that they are in control of their life.

Consider this story. A man of 102 was once asked during an interview to what he attributed his old age. He said he thought it was his mild manner and easy disposition. He went on to explain that on rising from bed each morning, he knows he has a choice to make: to be happy or not to be happy. He said he decided long ago that his choice was always to be happy, knowing that it made his life more interesting and much more enjoyable.

The concept that relates to our focus or reference point is known as our locus of control. Either we have an inner focus, an internal locus of control or an outer focus, an external locus of control. Where we place our focus has a lot to do with how we see ourselves, and how we act and react as we go about achieving our goals.

*All means prove
but a blunt instrument
if they have not behind them
a living spirit.*

ALBERT EINSTEIN
GERMAN-BORN PHYSICIST
(1879-1955)

A Strong Sense of Self

Every human being has as an inherent trait the desire to excel at something. It comes with our need to feel worthy, important and respected, both by ourselves and others. This desire we all have—to change, to grow and be worthy of respect—can be a mixed blessing, however. It can spur us on to dream great dreams, to accomplish great things, or to acquire great wealth. And if successful in such pursuits, we feel fulfilled as human beings.

But all such feelings are only temporary at best. They often last only as long as our last success. So we strive on for one success after another, hoping after hope that we'll be successful at least one more time. We need to understand that our well-being is being held hostage and is at great risk in this scenario, however, because sooner or later, Murphy's Law will pay us a visit—whatever can go wrong eventually will go wrong! That's just the way it is. Our number is bound to come up sometime.

When we do fail, we often begin to entertain negative thoughts and feelings. We feel unworthy, undeserving and unimportant—we feel unfulfilled as human beings. But it doesn't have to be this way if we have a strong SENSE OF SELF, and avoid linking either our successes or our failures in the material world directly to our self-worth and level of self-esteem.

Unfortunately, a great many people in today's materialistic world equate their total sense of self with their possessions and what they do for a living. The essence of our being is NOT our job, our home, our automobile, the size of our bank account, or even the body we occupy. These are merely external trappings, temporary circumstances at a particular point in time. We all enter this world naked and depart the same way, with not a little deterioration in our body during the interim. But our True Self doesn't change during our lifetime. **Who we are is represented in spirit.** It is our essence, our soul. It is a constant, never-ending. It is forever.

In the last analysis,
our only freedom
is the freedom
to discipline ourselves.

BERNARD BARUCH
AMERICAN FINANCIER AND STATESMAN
(1870-1965)

This battle, materialism versus spiritualism to find meaning in our life, is one we must wage every day. Many of our young people, thanks to slick advertising that capitalizes on our many weaknesses, have already lost the war. For it is human nature to be attracted to pleasurable things and repelled by painful things. The notion of deriving a positive sense of self through association with impressive objects is far more attractive than through association with who we really are. For most people have no idea who they really are, and lack the self-discipline and self-confidence to try to find out. The only game they know how to play is, "Hey, look what I have! And please ignore who I am."

So people get hooked on the notion that only through increased acquisitions can they prove to themselves and others that they are worthy and important. The fellow who drives the sleekest car and wears the latest fashions always gets the pretty girl! So what do many young men do? They quit school—to get a low paying job—to borrow the money—to buy the car. Now assume that a person has this car and quickly finds it doesn't live up to its billing. What happens? He feels even worse! He laments, "Since even this didn't work, I must really be a loser!" Of course, he believes it just didn't work for HIM. He still believes it works for everyone else!

The simple pursuit of wealth as a goal in and of itself will never result in fulfillment. The essence of living lies not in our GETTING—it lies in our GIVING. The law of mutual exchange says that we must always give in order to receive, that we define ourselves, indeed we FIND ourselves, through the contributions we make. And as we'll be discussing, this is not simple, altruistic advice. It is practical advice that reaps very real rewards.

By giving of ourselves in unselfish and significant ways, we become the richest person in the world. How "rich" do you think Mother Teresa thinks she is? If I were to guess at what her answer might be if asked this question, it would be something like this: "How rich am I? It is so large, it cannot be measured. There are so many people I can help—the sick, the poor, the lonely, the lost." Clearly she measures her wealth in terms of the CONTRIBUTION she can make. As Tolstoy has said, "We love people not for what they can do for us, but for what we can do for them."

*You can have
anything you want
if you want it
desperately enough.
You must want it
with an inner exuberance
that erupts through
the skin and joins the energy
that created the world.*

SHEILA GRAHAM
ENGLISH-BORN ACTRESS
AND JOURNALIST IN AMERICA
(1904-1988)

An Approach to Living

We know that no human being, if left to chance, is assured of success in any particular endeavour, despite our considerable intellectual powers. But I ask you—what if there was an approach you could follow that would dramatically increase your sense of self. Are feelings of high self-worth and high self-liking important to you?

If your answer is yes, then here's the approach I recommend:

> *Strive to become **excellent** at something you think is important and that intensely interests you.*

People act their best and feel their best when they're actively pursuing a goal they believe is important and is of great interest to them. There is no true labor in a labor of true love. It's done for the satisfaction inherent in it. All the fun is in the pursuit and not necessarily in the final outcome. People always gain something from the achievement process. They're all further ahead because they have risked and stretched—they have dared to test their outer limits.

Clearly, then, stretching and testing our outer limits is an important and necessary part of the achievement process. Otherwise, we can never hope to discover who we really are and what we're capable of achieving. As well, it's in discovering and doing something well over and over again that we find on-going reinforcement and positive feedback. It's reassuring to know that we are excellent at something, especially something that we think is important.

Where Are You Today?

Let's pose a few questions to set the stage and determine where you are today.

1. How well are you doing, in the various key aspects of your life? Let's do an inventory. Consider your personal health and fitness; your mental and spiritual health; family and other relationships;

*I think it's very important
to be positive
about everything in your life
that's negative.
You can turn a twist on it.*

BARBRA STREISAND
POPULAR AMERICAN SINGER

professionally; and financially. Look where you are today in these areas compared to where you were five years ago, and where you want to be five years from now.

2. Who is in charge of what's happening to you in your life? Are you, or is something outside you, in control? Until you decide that you're in charge and find out how to take control, I suggest you won't be able to bring about significant change in your life.

3. Do you know what you want out of life, all the good things you want? Do you know what success means to you? If it fell out of the sky today and landed on your doorstep, would you recognize it?

4. Do you know how to get all the things you want? Have you sought the advice of experts—through interviews, books, tapes and seminars—who have already succeeded in doing what you want to do?

5. What price are you willing to pay—in terms of time, effort and personal sacrifice—to get all the things you want? Are you willing to endure some short-term pain for long-term gain? Or is immediate gratification your primary preoccupation?

The objective of this book is to help you be the best you can be at whatever you attempt—to have total success in every aspect of your life. The means to this end can be simply stated: learn to use your brain in such a way that it empowers you rather than limits you. That is what this program offers: mental strategies to help you get the most out of yourself, and in turn the most out of your life. The trick is to *empower yourself!*—with empowering beliefs of your own potential and what you can accomplish, in spite of adversity, self-doubt, and repeated failure.

What does the term "empowerment" mean? Empowerment means "to enable yourself, to authorize yourself, to give power to yourself." More precisely, to be empowered means to have the ability to control your thoughts and actions in such a way that you get the precise results you want. It's the feeling you are in charge, that you are the instrument of change in your life. It's the ability to look at yourself in the mirror each morning and say, "Wow! Thank you, God, for another day to make a positive impact on the world."

*One
moment of
insight
is more valuable
than a life-time of
experience.*

WALTER STAPLES

Fundamentals

In this program, I discuss several fundamentals that are key to any success in your personal and professional life. We know it's the fundamentals at anything that lead to perfection. Whether it's architecture—like building a bridge; medicine—like performing heart surgery; or aerodynamics—like building an airplane; if the fundamentals of a particular science are not known and applied correctly, the results are always less than perfect. In fact, they're often disastrous! At one time or another, we've all heard about a bridge that collapsed, an operation that failed, or a plane that crashed.

But few people know the fundamentals of human behavior. Few of us know the answers to what I call the Five Ultimate Questions:

1. Who am I?
2. How did I get this way?
3. Why do I think, feel and behave the way I do?
4. Can I change, improve for the better?
5. And the most important question of all—HOW?

Most of us are represented by the lyrics in the rock song that say, "We're working on the mysteries without any clues."

To understand how we can improve, we have to understand how the mind works. Now you might say it isn't important how the mind works. After all, we seem to get along without knowing a whole lot about many things—how a car works, for example. Yet we still drive cars, and more often than not we get where we want to go.

But consider this. An experienced mechanic can make a car literally hum. He can make it more fuel efficient. In fact, he can make an average car outperform a more powerful car—simply by fine-tuning its engine. So we see that a mechanic who knows the intimate functioning of his instrument can make it perform at its optimum. But how many of us are functioning at our optimum today in the way we think and in the way we perform—in the way we run our brain and central nervous system?

*My philosophy is that
not only are you responsible
for your life,
but doing the best
at this moment
puts you in the best place
for the next moment.*

OPRAH WINFREY
POPULAR AMERICAN TALK-SHOW HOST

We Live by Choice

TO THINK—it's our ability to think that separates us from all other living creatures on earth. Creatures are born with instincts pre-programmed into their very being, instincts that they are neither aware of nor able to change, but instincts that nonetheless represent a success system. A duck is a duck, and can be nothing but a duck. But we all know that every duck is very good at being a duck. All ducks quack, swim, procreate and fly south every winter, and never have to think about it. They just do it!

The thinking engaged in by humans is vastly different than that engaged in by animals. We function by free choice rather than rote instinct. Our range of possibilities knows no limits. We are free to learn, grow, experiment and create. We have a brain with a spark of intellect. We know we have choices, and that a particular choice will result in a particular consequence. We can contemplate our existence on this earth and what may be in store for us in the hereafter. We have the power to be whoever we want to be and do whatever we want to do. As Ralph Waldo Emerson, the noted American philosopher once commented, "So far as a man *thinks,* he is free."

But how many of us are as successful at running our brains as ducks are at running theirs? Ducks don't seem confused about who they are. They all seem to know exactly what to do. And they all seem to be happy with their current state of affairs—with the way they think!

What if we were to ask ourselves the question, "Do I feel totally happy and fulfilled today as a result of the way I think?" For the vast majority of us, our answer would be a resounding "No!" The only recourse available to us, then, is to master our thought processes so we get more of what we want rather than what we don't want. Remember, winning is an inner game, a state of mind. And each of us can develop our mind . . . but first we must want to do it, then take the time to do it. So let's continue our study of the process of human thought.

Personally,
I'm always ready
to learn,
although I do not always like
being taught.

WINSTON CHURCHILL
FORMER PRIME MINISTER OF ENGLAND
(1874-1965)

YOU HAVE TO SET YOURSELF ON F-I-R-E!

TOM DEMPSEY

Tom Dempsey was born with only half a right foot and a deformed right arm. But he didn't let his handicap deter him. At a young age, he had an idea, a dream really. He wanted to be a football player—specifically, a field-goal kicker. He began by playing football in high school and college, and did reasonably well. By this time, his dream had grown to much larger proportions—he now wanted to be a *professional* football player.

Few people took Tom seriously, including the many scouts for the professional football teams. Surely he was not being realistic. After repeated rejection, however, the New Orleans Saints finally decided to give him a tryout. And he made the team!

His big moment to prove himself came on November 8, 1970. The Saints were leading the Detroit Lions by a score of 17 to 16, with just 17 seconds left in the game. Then Detroit kicked a field goal and went up 19 to 17. The Saints took the kick-off. Two plays later, with only 2 seconds left on the clock, they were still on their own 37 yard line—63 yards from Detroit's end-zone. What could they do? They decided to kick a field goal, and Tom Dempsey trotted onto the field.

The record for a field goal at the time was 56 yards. Was it possible to kick an extra 7 yards—fully 21 additional feet? Tom Dempsey kicked a 63-yard field goal, and his name went into the record books. He still holds the record today.

You make a difference by giving something of yourself for the betterment of others. Tom Dempsey has made a difference. He dared to dream big dreams, and in the process, he set himself on fire!

*The greater danger
for most of us
is not that our aim is
too high
and we miss it,
but that it is
too low
and we reach it.*

MICHELANGELO
ITALIAN PAINTER, SCULPTOR,
ARCHITECT AND POET
(1475-1564)

CHAPTER 3

We Create Our Own Reality

The mind is its own place, and in itself
can make a heav'n of Hell a hell of Heav'n.
—John Milton

The Learning Process

We come to a discussion of the learning process as it applies to all human beings, how the conscious and subconscious parts of our mind work together. First, we operate at the **unconscious incompetence** level—we don't know that we don't know how to do something. When we discover that we don't know that we don't know, we're at the **conscious incompetence** level. If we then learn how to do something, albeit with some difficulty, we move to the **conscious competence** level. And after the learning process has been fully ingrained, we're at the **unconscious competence** level—we don't even know anymore that we know how to do something. We just do it automatically, like driving to work every day or tying our shoelaces.

Again, we move from

unconscious incompetence, to
conscious incompetence, to
conscious competence, to
unconscious competence.

Understanding and applying this process to the way we think is critical to all self-improvement and meaningful change. First we have to be shown and told that we're not very competent in the way we're now running our brain, thus moving to the conscious incompetent level, and then be taught a better way, how to be consciously competent. When we practice thinking more effectively over and over again, we slowly move from the conscious competent mode to the unconscious competent mode. Then it's like being on automatic pilot all over again. Only this time, we're functioning at our very best.

*The definition of success
is getting many of the things
money can buy—and all the things
money can't buy.*

ZIG ZIGLAR
MOTIVATIONAL SPEAKER
AND AUTHOR OF
SEE YOU AT THE TOP

What Is Success?

In the context of being our best, of wanting to be happier and to get more out of life, BETA Research of Syosset, N.Y., recently surveyed 2,000 men and women, and asked what they would most like to change, if they could. Here are their answers, in order of priority:

> 1. More financial security. 2. Enjoy better health. 3. Achieve greater success. 4. Enhance home life. 5. Improve appearance. 6. Improve education. 7. Better family relationships. 8. Increase relaxation. 9. Enhance life-style. 10. Better outlook on life.

From this list, we see that everyone wants more of something. And this is exactly what "success" is: success is the ongoing process of becoming more, of developing all aspects of our full potential. But first we have to BE more—develop ourselves both mentally and spiritually—before we can DO more before we can HAVE more. The world is full of people who want above-average results without willing to become above-average people. And it just isn't possible.

Here is an insightful observation by Margaret Young: "Often people attempt to live their lives backwards; they try to HAVE more things or more money, in order to DO more of what they want, so they will BE happier. The way it actually works is the reverse. You first must BE who you really are, then DO what you need to do, in order to HAVE what you want."

Happiness!

Man eternally has been in search of happiness. William James, the famous American psychologist, identified this universal trait long ago when he wrote, "If we were to ask the question, 'What is life's chief concern?' one of the answers we should receive would be: 'It is happiness.' How to gain, how to keep, how to recover happiness is in fact the secret motive of all we do, and all we are willing to endure." And William Butler Yeats, the Irish essayist and poet, added this insight: "Happiness is neither virtue nor pleasure nor this thing nor that, but simply GROWTH. We are happy when we are growing."

*This one thing I know:
the only ones among you
who will be really happy
are those who will have
sought and found how
to serve.*

ALBERT SCHWEITZER
ALSATIAN THEOLOGIAN, MUSICIAN
AND MISSIONARY
(1875-1965)

All the rewards we receive in life—both emotional and material—are a function of how well we tap into and develop our full potential. Our potential is a function of three primary ingredients: our natural talents; our personal belief system; and our inner desire. All three must be present and mutually self- supporting if we're ever to achieve the performance we aspire to and rightfully deserve.

For example, we can have plenty of talent and a lot of desire, but still lack belief. The result is not significant. Or we can have a lot of talent and firm belief, but still lack desire. Again, the result is not significant. Or we can have limited talent, coupled with strong desire and strong belief. The result in this case is often very significant. There are many examples, from professional athletes to business tycoons to world leaders to everyday people, where the most successful are not the most talented or the most gifted people. They are the ones with the most desire and the most belief. They are the ones that have done their best with what they were given to work with, and have reaped the appropriate rewards.

The Staples Principle

The late Dr. Laurence Peter, the noted Canadian-born author and educator, is known around the world for his famous "Peter Principle." The Peter Principle says that you rise to your level of incompetence. This phenomenon does seem to apply to the vast majority of people—those who live their life according to chance rather than choice. They don't accept the notion that continuous improvement and constant learning must never end.

Yet we all know this principle doesn't apply to everyone. There is a more universal principle that does, although only a select few fully understand it and apply it in their daily life. This is the principle—the Staples Principle. It should be inscribed in every book of learning, etched into the mind of every student and business person who hopes to achieve anything of significance:

You'll always rise
in life
to the level of responsibility
that you're willing
to accept.

RALPH WALDO EMERSON
AMERICAN ESSAYIST, PHILOSOPHER
AND POET
(1803-1882)

You rise to the level of competence
you aspire to and prepare yourself for.

We know the will to win is nothing without the will **to prepare** *to win*. Abraham Lincoln as a young man vowed, "I will always try to do my best no matter what, and some day my chance will come." The Optimists Club has an interesting saying: "The future belongs to those who prepare for it." And Zig Ziglar says, "If you're easy on yourself, life will be hard on you; but if you're hard on yourself, life will be easy on you." The question is, which way would you rather have it?

Life Is . . .

What is life? Learned people have been trying to answer this question for centuries. Here is one way it could be described: "Life is like a dog-sled team. If you're not the lead dog and always breaking new ground, your view of the world never changes!" (In other words, all you ever see is the rear-end of the dog in front!) And Rosalind Russell commented in one of her movies, "Life is like a banquet table. But there are always some poor suckers who still manage to starve to death."

Here is my answer to the question "What is life?"—**life is . . . a series of thoughts.** Incredibly simple, isn't it? That's only FOUR WORDS! We must understand that it's our thoughts that make us who we are and the world appear to us as it appears. We are today where our thoughts have brought us. And we'll be tomorrow where our thoughts take us. If our thoughts don't change, NOTHING in our life can change.

This quotation from the Pali Canon, which are ancient Buddhist scriptures dated between 500 and 250 B.C., is remarkable in its insight. It says, "All that is comes from the mind; it is based on the mind; it is fashioned by the mind."

"All that is." That would seem to include quite a few things, I'm sure you'll agree. Our *mind*—and our mind alone—creates our reality. Nothing really IS. It is only what our mind decides IS.

*I know of no more
encouraging fact
than the unquestionable
ability of man
to elevate his life
by conscious effort.*

HENRY DAVID THOREAU
AMERICAN NATURALIST, PHILOSOPHER
AND WRITER
(1817-1862)

This introduces the important concept of "first cause." In humans, we have seen that everything begins with thought. Hence THOUGHT IS FIRST CAUSE. Everything else is a follow-on effect. Later on, we'll discuss where thoughts come from.

Our Personal Belief System

The world operates on the basis of cause and effect. It's the master law of the universe. It says that for every action or effect, there is first a prior cause. In the human system, our thoughts are the cause—and our behavior and circumstances are the effect. Clearly life is a mental adventure, not a physical journey. It is our thought processes we must focus on and ultimately improve upon.

If we want to exercise more control over our thoughts in order to become more competent, more productive and more fulfilled, we must understand how our mind works.

The total accumulation of data involving everything that has ever happened to us in our life is referred to as our personal belief system, our reality or the truth as we know, understand and accept it to be. It serves as our frame of reference as we continue to experience new things in life and represents the total "programming" our mind has been subjected to, voluntarily or involuntarily, up to now.

For example, who we are at this very moment, whatever we happen to be doing, is what our mind **believes** we are. Our abilities to solve a problem, perform a task or reach a specific goal all depend on our mind's stored beliefs about our strengths and weaknesses in each of these areas.

The breakthrough comes when we realize that many parts of the belief system we now have are totally unreliable since they are based on information that is often inaccurate, insufficient or irrational. Few of us really "know" that much about anything, even in this modern age, especially about our own inherent talents and abilities that rarely have been fully and properly tested. People acquire their beliefs from their prior experiences—or more correctly, from their interpretation of these prior experiences. Therefore any particular belief we may now have is more of a subjective opinion than an

*Everything in Nature
contains all the power
of Nature.
Everything is made
of one hidden stuff.*

RALPH WALDO EMERSON
AMERICAN ESSAYIST, PHILOSOPHER
AND POET
(1803-1882)

objective fact. Only by the critical reassessment of long-standing beliefs can we change them and move ahead with our life. This necessarily involves doing some serious thinking, in fact, some serious RE-thinking!

The Mirroring Effect

One of the most important concepts regarding personal empowerment relates to what I call the Mirroring Effect. The Mirroring Effect says that *our outer world is* **always** *a reflection of our inner world,* of the type of thoughts, words and pictures we have in our head. It represents a major tool we can use to bring about a perceptual transformation in our life. A perceptual transformation refers to seeing in the world around us "what might be" as compared to what actually "seems to be there." When we begin to see what can't be seen, and ardently believe it, then things really begin to happen!

This begs the question, "What determines the type of thoughts, words and pictures we have in our head?" This of course depends on the frame of reference or perspective from which we view the world, what we previously described as our locus of control. People mirror back to the world either from "the inside out" or "the outside in."

People who have an inner focus, who operate from an internal frame of reference and a strong set of core beliefs, **are able to see in the world around them precisely what they believe.** It should be no surprise that such people see opportunity, abundance, health, wealth and happiness everywhere they look. They mirror from "the inside out," and create this as their reality. They have an internal locus of control.

Other people who have an outer focus, who operate from an external frame of reference and a weak set of core beliefs, always mirror in reverse. **They have chosen to believe what they see in the world around them—**and what do they see? They see apathy, pessimism, lack, doubt, fear and failure everywhere they look. And where do they look? They look in the newspapers, the tabloid headlines, and

To live content with small means;
to seek elegance rather than luxury,
and refinement rather than fashion;
to be worthy, not respectable,
and wealthy, not rich;
to study hard, think quietly,
talk gently, act frankly;
to listen to stars and birds,
to babes and sages, with open heart;
to bear all cheerfully, do all bravely,
await occasions, hurry never.
In a word, to let the spiritual,
unbidden and unconscious,
grow up through the common.
This is to be my symphony.

WILLIAM CHANNING
AMERICAN CLERGYMAN, AUTHOR
AND PHILANTHROPIST
(1780-1842)

the TV news where they are bombarded with the recession, the lay-offs, the crime, the drugs, the violence and the despair that are all around them. They mirror what they see in the world, and bring these same messages into their life and create this as their reality. They have an external locus of control.

Think of it. **Either we see what we believe,** knowing we can control what we believe; **or we believe what we see,** knowing we have no control over what we see.

U. S. Andersen provides a more detailed explanation of this fascinating concept in his wonderful book *The Magic in Your Mind:*

> We exist in order that we may become something more than we are, not through favorable circumstance or auspicious occurrence, but through an inner search for increased awareness. To be, to become, these are the commandments of evolving life, which is going somewhere, aspires to some unscaled heights, and the awakened soul answers the call, seeks, grows, expands. To do less is to sink into the reactive prison of the ego, with all its pain, suffering, limitation, decay, and death. The man who lives through reaction to the world around him is the victim of every change in his environment, now happy, now sad, now victorious, now defeated, affected but never affecting. He may live many years in this manner, rapt with sensory perception and the ups and downs of his surface self, but one day pain so outweighs pleasure that he suddenly perceives his ego is illusory, a product of outside circumstances only. Then he either sinks into complete animal lethargy or, turning away from the senses, seeks inner awareness and self-mastery. Then he is on the road to really living, truly becoming; then he begins to uncover his real potential; then he discovers the miracle of his own consciousness, the magic in his mind.

To what extent are we affected by "messages" from our environment? *U.S. News and World Report* says that young adults currently in grades 9 to 12 will see an average of 18,000 murders watching 22,000 hours of television. This is about one murder every 45 minutes! And the 22,000 hours of television are more than twice the time spent in class during 12 full years of schooling.

*The recipe for perpetual
ignorance is to be satisfied
with your opinions
and content with your knowledge.*

ELBERT HUBBARD
AMERICAN WRITER
(1856-1915)

A study released in March 1993 by the American Psychological Association says that some children are seeing so much fictionalized violence that they are becoming desensitized to the implications of real violence. For example, a child watching two to four hours of television a day will have seen 8,000 murders and 100,000 acts of violence *before* reaching high school, says the study.

By the end of the teenage years, a young person will have witnessed more than 200,000 acts of television violence, a figure that is steadily increasing with the availability of pay-TV and video movies such as Die Hard 2 (which depicts 264 deaths), Robocop (81 deaths), and Total Recall (74 deaths).

It should be no surprise that this kind of programming has a powerful and lasting impact on young, impressionable minds and helps explain the explosion in crime and acts of violence among teenagers today.

The following cartoon gives us a chilling yet accurate depiction of how young people are programmed and pre-conditioned by our environment to act in negative and unproductive ways.

If you always aim low in life, you'll keep shooting yourself in the foot.

WALTER STAPLES

Good timber
does not grow
with ease;
the stronger the wind,
the stronger the trees.

J. WILLARD MARRIOTT
FOUNDER OF MARRIOTT HOTELS
(1900-1985)

So either our strong inner beliefs become our reality or the outer world becomes our reality. And whatever becomes our reality becomes the driving force in our life. Here's the relevant question to ask yourself: "Am I alive and active and having an impact on the world, or is the world alive and active and having an impact on me?" We are all like puppets on a stage. The question is, who is pulling the strings?

Enlightened and determined people reflect their inner beliefs upon the outside world. They are in control by virtue of their firm beliefs. They march to the beat of their own drum. Passive people reflect the outside world onto their internal belief system. They are out of control by virtue of the mixed messages the world sends them. External factors determine the beat of their drum.

Exercise

Here is an exercise to give you some insight into your locus of control, to see whether it tends to be internal or external. There are eight questions. Determine your answer to each question on the basis of what you personally now believe, either YES or NO, and place it in the column at the right.

*If you go by other people's opinions
or predictions, you'll just end up
talking yourself out of something.
If you're running down the track of life
thinking that it's impossible to break
life's records, those thoughts have a
funny way of sinking into your feet.*

CARL LEWIS
U.S. OLYMPIC CHAMPION

LOCUS OF CONTROL QUIZ

Do you believe . . .	YES	NO	SCORE
1. you succeed in life largely as a result of your own efforts?	___	___	___
2. making a lot of money is mainly a matter of luck?	___	___	___
3. by your words and actions, you can influence others in positive and predictable ways?	___	___	___
4. it is who you know, not what you know, that gets you ahead?	___	___	___
5. getting along with others is a skill you can learn?	___	___	___
6. if you haven't "made it" by age 40, you never will?	___	___	___
7. if people had helped you more, you would be further ahead in life?	___	___	___
8. it is your past that is holding you back from being successful today?	___	___	___

This raises a disturbing question: if my perception is just a bundle of random experiences in response to a basically random world, how real am I?

—Deepak Chopra, M.D., *Unconditional Life*

*We must select the illusion
that appeals
to our temperament and
embrace it with passion,
if we want to be happy.*

CYRIL CONNOLLY
ENGLISH ESSAYIST, CRITIC
AND NOVELIST
(1903-1974)

Answers

1. YES   2. NO   3. YES   4. NO   5. YES   6. NO   7. NO   8. NO

Score two points for a correct answer and one point for an incorrect answer. Add up the total. Determine your personal locus of control from the box below.

TOTAL	LOCUS OF CONTROL
15-16	HIGH INTERNAL
13-14	LOW INTERNAL
10-12	LOW EXTERNAL
8-9	HIGH EXTERNAL

Explanation

Consider whether the causal factor in each of these questions is internal to an individual or external. You cannot control the external—luck, your age, your past or other people. You can only control the internal—your own words, thoughts, feelings, actions and behavior; in other words, your own reality.

The Power of Perception

What is "reality," anyway? To help answer this question, let me quote from the book *Beyond Biofeedback* by Elmer and Alyce Green:

No one has ever seen the outside world. All that we can be aware of are our interpretations of the electrical patterns in the brain. Our only view of the world is on our own living internal television screen. The occipital (visual) cortex is essentially the screen and the eyes are two cameras that give us information about the frequencies and intensities of light. When the eyes are open, we say we are looking at the world, but it is the occipital cortex that we actually "look" at. What we see are millions of brain cells firing in appropriate ways to display the retinal activity.

*What if everything
is an illusion
and nothing exists?
In that case,
I definitely overpaid
for my carpet.*

WOODY ALLEN
AMERICAN DIRECTOR AND ACTOR

Let's explore the concept that we create our own reality—true or false, positive or negative, desirable or undesirable—in our mind. Clearly our physical senses are quite unreliable instruments when it comes to perceiving our world accurately. We know many animals and birds that can see, hear or smell much better than we humans can.

As an example, imagine sailing in a boat along the equator, traveling due east. As you proceed in this direction and assuming you didn't know any different, your eyes would tell you that you're traveling in a flat, straight line. Of course, you're not, as we all know. You would be traveling in a complete circle, for you would eventually end up exactly where you started.

Or consider what you see when you look at a set of train tracks that stretch off into the distance, and seemingly come together at the horizon. But do train tracks ever come together? Of course not. They're exactly four feet, eight and a half inches apart—ALWAYS!— at least in North America. Clearly if we didn't know any better, this incorrect information received through our senses would become our reality.

Now imagine you were zipping along on a train, looked ahead and concluded that the train tracks did come together, and therefore the train you were on was certain to crash. So you immediately JUMP OFF, knowing this is the only way to avoid almost certain death. Obviously such drastic action is not required. And this is what a lot of us do in our life. We jump off a given path we're on to avoid what we perceive to be a negative outcome. The key word is "perceive." Obviously we are limited physically from seeing things in the world as they actually are.

Another way we create our own reality is through what is called "selective perception." We tend to read into an event what our screening system decides at a given point in time is of primary importance to us. What is important is a function of our current dominant thoughts. For example, consider what different people "see" when they look out a window and observe a wet, rainy day.

One person, a farmer concerned about his crop during a dry

ℌell begins on the day when God
grants us a clear vision of all
that we might have achieved, of all
the gifts which we have wasted, of all
that we might have done
which we did not do.
For me the conception of Hell lies
in two words: TOO LATE.

GIAN CARLO MENOTTI
ITALIAN-BORN COMPOSER
AND DRAMATIST IN AMERICA

spell, looks out and sees the promise of a better harvest. He is pleased with what he "sees." Another, a weather forecaster, looks out and sees the beginning of a broad low front sweeping in from the north-west, exactly as she had predicted. Based on barometer settings, the speed of the wind, temperature and humidity, she must begin to prepare another forecast. She is preoccupied with what she "sees."

A third person, a young man courting his true love, looks out and sees his well-planned day as a total disaster. He was hoping to have a picnic with his fiancée in a quiet spot near a stream. He is disappointed with what he "sees." A scientist, studying acid rain and its effects on local fish stocks, looks out and decides that it's an ideal time to take more water samples in the nearby lake. She is excited with what she "sees."

In these examples, everyone physically saw EXACTLY THE SAME THING when he or she looked out the window. Yet each one made different interpretations and came to different conclusions based on the same information. There is an important lesson to be learned from these examples, and it is this:

> **The world itself is a neutral place.** No single event in and of itself is either positive or negative. IT JUST IS!

It remains then for each of us to decide what is the appropriate label to place on each event. Clearly, the more varied interpretations we can make and place on specific events in our life, whether such events initially appear good or bad, positive or negative, desirable or undesirable, the more successful we'll be at responding to and conquering life's many challenges.

Hidden Prompters at Work

The same process applies when we look at and "see" ourselves in the context of various goals we're striving for. Our five senses—what we use to see, hear, smell, taste and touch—look out at the world, and give us a sense of who we are and what we can accomplish. If we decide, consciously, that we can do something, then our Subconscious Mind accepts this as fact and begins to bring it into reality.

Be bold—
and mighty forces will
come to your aid.

BASIL KING
AMERICAN RELIGIOUS WRITER
(1859-1928)

Positive hidden prompters are major players and aid us in this task. They pop up with their cue cards and say, "Yes, you can do this and this and this. So get on with the job."

The same thing happens if we decide that we cannot do something. The Subconscious Mind brings this negative outcome into reality as well. Again hidden prompters, this time all negative, jump up and say, "Don't be silly. You can't do this or this or this. Give up now and don't waste your time." The job of the Subconscious Mind is clear and straightforward: **it is always to create according to the "truth" that is presented to it.**

Of course, in many cases the hidden prompters provide conflicting advice. The positives present their point of view as do the negatives, both sides frantically trying to win us over. The argument in our mind can go on forever. In the end, the set of beliefs that dominates will prevail. And the Subconscious Mind will act accordingly.

What we need to avoid at all costs is to let messages from the physical world dictate to us who we are and what we can aspire to be, do and have in our life. For example, if you received 100—or 500— "no's" trying to market a new product or service you created and perfected, does this automatically mean you should throw in the towel and pursue another line of work? Colonel Sanders of Kentucky Fried Chicken fame didn't. He received more than 1,000 "no's" before he got his first "yes" trying to sell his personal recipe for cooking chicken. Few of us could endure such repeated rejection. His approach seems to have been, "I'm only in the 'yes' business. So I'll just keep on until that's what I find."

Or consider what Michelangelo, Columbus, Einstein, Edison, Alexander Graham Bell, Marconi, Ford or the Wright brothers all had in common. Each was labelled at one time or another in their life as either an idiot, an incompetent or a dreamer. And there may well be a grain of truth in some of these accusations. After all, you have to be a little crazy if you think being a bicycle repairman qualifies you to build and fly an airplane! But the fact remains, these men persevered and were not distracted by their detractors from what they "knew" they could do.

*There is no meaning
to life
except the meaning
man gives his life
by the unfolding of
his powers.*

ERICH FROMM
GERMAN-BORN PSYCHOANALYST
AND SOCIAL PHILOSOPHER
(1900-1980)

In other words, should you let the market's initial reaction to your product or service define who you are and your level of success as a person? Or is something negative or unflattering that your father, mother, a teacher, a friend or employer said to you at one time or another relevant to who you really are? Of course not. Such feedback is simply other people's opinions based on their subjective interpretation of isolated facts and limited information.

In trying to find a publisher for my book *Think Like a Winner!* I was turned down by eight different firms, many of them the largest and most prestigious publishers in the United States. But if I took their response as defining my relative level of success as an author and gave up, the book would never have been published. The book is now available in six languages in over 35 countries around the world.

We Live in a Mental World

Here's a statement of fact, if you give it some thought:

> To change the world as we now know it and understand it,
> we need only perceive it in a different light.

In other words, we need to experience a perceptual transformation of who we are in the context of the world at large. We must understand that **we live in a mental world,** not a physical one. All our five senses can do is give us tiny bits of information, an impression, from the outside world that we can interpret in a myriad of ways. It isn't that what we need to see in order to be successful is always "invisible" to the human eye. It's just that often we're not able to see it in our "mind's eye"—our view from within—how we interpret the information we receive. People whose inner power of vision transcends the stimuli of the outer world are in charge of the reality they create. Since they're in charge, they are also in control. As Anthony Robbins has noted, "As long as we structure our lives in a way that our happiness is dependent upon something we cannot control, then we will experience pain."

It is
the chiefest point
of happiness that a man
is willing to be
what he is.

DESIDERIUS ERASMUS
DUTCH HUMANIST, THEOLOGIAN
AND WRITER
(1466-1536)

We all create our own reality—in our mind. And what we choose to see and focus on is what we get. Whatever dominates—by way of the words and pictures and images in our mind—is in control. We have to believe it—before we can "see" it—before we can do it—before we can have it in our life. In a phrase: **believing is seeing!** The better known phrase, seeing is believing, is not always true. Remember the train tracks!

We always relate what is happening in the outside world to our personal belief system, to what we believe we can or cannot accomplish in our life. If we believe there is no limit to what we can accomplish, then this is the perspective from which we view the world and everything that's going on in it. **The outer world will always be a reflection of our inner mind.** So we must ensure that our mind has an accurate and realistic sense of our True Self.

> Human beings, by changing the inner aspects of their minds, can change the outer aspects of their lives.
>
> —William James

Understanding this, we see that life is really an inner game. Because as we think, so we are. We will always bring into our life whatever we think about the most, believe the most, expect the most and imagine the most. And this will happen whether we want it to or not. But once we understand that this is how the mind works, we can begin to see the incredible choices that are available to us—what to think, what to believe, what to expect and what to imagine!

The True Self

This brings us to an explanation of the **True Self.** We were born as perfect beings with perfect intelligence. We are perfect copies from a master blueprint with infinite powers to ponder, create, imagine and act. But what happens? After birth, we experience something of life—thoughts, ideas and events—that gives us an interpretation, a sense, a superficial understanding of who we think we are. We then grow up with this false impression of ourselves firmly imbedded in our Subconscious Mind, and we act out this false impression for the rest of our lives. In the process, we create an arbitrary and inaccurate self, an unrealistic self that I call our **Artificial Self,** and never fully acquire a true understanding of who we really are.

The great aim
of education
is not knowledge
but action.

HERBERT SPENCER
ENGLISH PHILOSOPHER
(1820-1903)

Our Artificial Self is a product of our senses and life-time experiences in the physical world. It represents our current self-image that has as its basis past judgments about sensory inputs. It is our false ego that forever tells us we're superior to some and inferior to others, but always less than our True Self. Our True Self is well hidden and will always be unknown to us. But we can learn more about who we really are through introspection and imagination, and by taking focused ACTION in the direction of our goals.

Any thoughts of inferiority we may have are total delusion. They have no basis in reality. They are simply a result of a conspiracy of our senses. It's a cheap and dirty trick we play on ourselves, and we don't deserve such treatment. But to undo it, we have to start all over again and rethink who we really are. As Emerson once said, "There are no great and no small." In other words, we all have the potential for greatness, for accomplishing whatever it is we want to accomplish, if only we can free ourselves from our preconceived ideas and self-limiting beliefs. And so this must be our point of departure, where we begin.

Our Area of Excellence

A concept that gives us a better idea of who we really are is known as our area of excellence. This concept says each of us has, on average, the same talents and abilities that everyone else has. In other words, we're slightly better at doing some things—for example, better at driving a car, at cooking and telling jokes; and slightly worse at other things—worse at tennis, at remembering names and drawing pictures. When averaged all together, our average equates to just about everyone else's average.

However, this concept also says that we all possess the ability to excel in at least one key area of our life. Each of us was put on earth for a specific purpose, and with the necessary talents and abilities consistent with this purpose. This means we can all excel at something, and it is our primary responsibility to find our area of excellence, what we are really good at, and to channel all of our efforts

*A*NTHROPOMAXIMOLOGY:
the study of
the upper limits
of human potential.

ANONYMOUS

in this direction. Our area of excellence is usually something that naturally interests us, that we are instinctively attracted to, and that we would perform whether we were paid to do it or not. The activity makes us feel unique, valuable and important as human beings. It helps us define who we really are, and allows us to express our distinctiveness and individuality.

One way to tell if you have found your area of excellence is to ask yourself these two questions:

1. Do you feel ecstatic about what you are doing on a regular basis?
2. Do you find you are surprised at your level of performance on a regular basis?

If you are not ecstatic about what you're doing and surprised with your level of performance on a regular basis, then you haven't found your area of excellence. And this search, this undertaking, is without doubt the most important task that faces each of us in our life. It is our mightiest challenge. Yes, we can pretend it isn't important to do right now. After all, there is a lot of time and we'll get around to it eventually. Or we can pretend it doesn't matter. We'll still get by, in our own way. BUT TIME IS OF THE ESSENCE AND IT REALLY DOES MATTER . . . if we want to discover and bring out the very best that is in us, if we want to leave something behind that is significant, our mark in the sand, if you will . . . something that has a life and a purpose all of its own that goes on and on . . . even after we ourselves are dead and gone.

Man's search for meaning in fact is a search for Truth—of who we really are.

*It's good to be just plain happy,
it's a little better to know that
you're happy; but to understand that
you're happy and to know why and how
and still be happy—be happy in the being
and the knowing—well, that is beyond
happiness, that is bliss.*

HENRY MILLER
AMERICAN WRITER
(1891-1980)

YOU HAVE TO SET YOURSELF ON F-I-R-E!

A. L. WILLIAMS

Art Lynch Williams is president of one of the fastest-growing companies in business history. But he doesn't look the part. Born and raised in a small town in south Georgia, he didn't attend an ivy league school or earn a business degree. He says he's lousy at math and spelling. And by his own admission, he is short, a little overweight and hates business suits, preferring instead casual attire that he wore in his previous career as an award-winning high school football coach.

In 1977, A.L. founded a business with 85 associates selling term life insurance. By 1987, only 10 years later, his company had sold $81.4 billion (note **billion**) in individual life insurance policies. How did all this happen? This is a story A.L. loves to tell. He believes it offers hope and encouragement to all the so-called "ordinary" people in life who think—wrongly—that they don't have what it takes to succeed. He believes that such things as I.Q., level of education and social standing are not the keys to success . . . but that finding a dream consistent with your beliefs and values is. As he says, "Dreams are the fuel that fire desire."

During the first two years in business, A.L. states categorically that "the thing that kept me going was this big dream of being financially independent. There's no possibility of winning if you don't have a big dream." His values are also a key part of his business success. He believes organizations should help business people succeed where it really counts—in their family lives. "I'm absolutely convinced that you can't separate your personal, family and spiritual life from your business life," A.L. says. "If you're lousy in one of those first areas, you'll be lousy in business, too. So (in our business) we try to talk to people about priorities and having a balanced life." These ideas have helped make A.L. and many of his salespeople multi-millionaires.

You make a difference by giving something of yourself for the betterment of others. A.L. Williams has made a difference. He dared to dream big dreams, and in the process, he set himself on fire!

There isn't a thing I can't do now
that I couldn't do when I was 18 . . .
I did nothing when I was 18 . . .
I was even worse when I was 17 . . .
I wasn't so hot when I was 25 either.
I saved everything for now.
I hate to brag, but I'm very good at it now.

GEORGE BURNS
AMERICAN COMEDIAN
(1896-1996)

CHAPTER 4

Think, Re-think,
Then Think Again

If error is corrected whenever it is recognized as such,
the path of error is the path of truth.
—Hans Reichenbach

The Sensory Stimulus Trap

We now come to the core concept that relates to the psychology
of the self. I call it the Sensory Stimulus Trap. It explains how our
ability to take action is a function of our sense of self that comes from
two primary inputs. Let's call them Input A and Input B.

INPUT A: How we see ourselves as a result of the mixed messages
the physical world regularly sends us. This is the Brahman method:
the truth discovered objectively through observation.

INPUT B: How we see ourselves in light of our conception of our
True Self, and as an extension of a higher power. This describes the
Atman method: the truth discovered subjectively through intro-
spection.

These are the two sources, and only sources, from which we can
access information and make a final determination. It is critical on
our part to make proper judgments and come to the right conclusion about who we really are—our True Self.

*It is the commonest of mistakes
to consider that the limit
of our power of perception
is also the limit of
all there is to perceive.*

C. W. LEADBEATER
AMERICAN AUTHOR
(1847-1934)

THE SENSORY STIMULUS TRAP

FIGURE 1

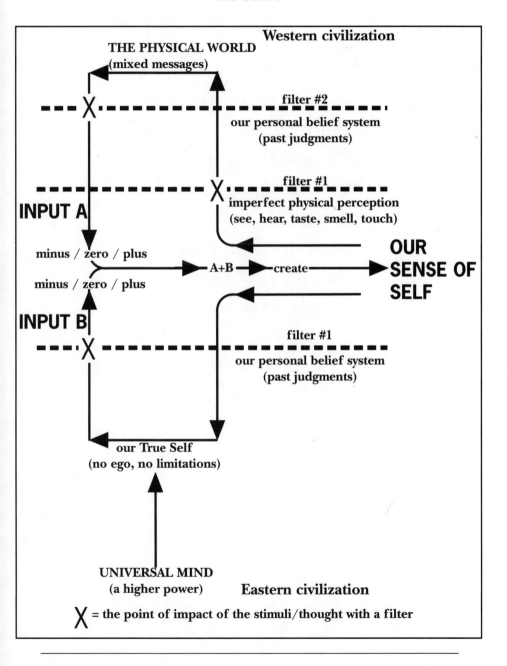

*The mind, in proportion
as it is cut off from free
communication with nature,
with revelation, with God,
with itself, loses its life,
just as the body droops
when debarred from the
air and the cheering
light from heaven.*

WILLIAM CHANNING
AMERICAN CLERGYMAN,
AUTHOR AND PHILANTHROPIST
(1780-1842)

In more detail, here is what is happening.

Input A

We look out at the physical world using our five senses to gain a sense of who we are. Three errors occur as we receive the messages:

1. Since our sensors are imperfect devices, they cannot perceive the world as it really is. Hence we sense only part of what is actually there. This is filter #1. Result: the information is limited.

2. The physical world always sends us mixed messages. In fact, IT CAN ONLY SEND US MIXED MESSAGES because that is what is going on. Therefore there is no consistency to our inputs to help us decide one way or another who we really are. Result: the information is inconsistent.

3. We must filter whatever messages we do receive through the personal belief system we already have. This is filter #2. Therefore we interpret them and tend to color them based on past judgments. Result: the information is biased.

Because of these three very real limitations inherent in the sensory perception process—accessing information that is all at once limited, inconsistent and biased—it is impossible to get a realistic sense of our True Self from looking solely at the physical world. If this is the only basis we use to make up our mind, we are doomed, totally and completely, and we'll never know.

Input B

Through introspection and contemplation, we can look inward into the spiritual side of our nature, and try to conceptualize our True Self. Then we can compare our findings with what we already believe about ourselves from other sources—filter #1—and update our belief system. We know we are creations of a higher power, of a force much greater than ourselves. And this power has endowed us with the ability to imagine our future, to consider our possibilities,

*When the fight begins
within himself, a
man's worth something.*

ROBERT BROWNING
ENGLISH POET
(1812-1889)

and to explore our full potential. We know "believing is seeing," hence our limitations do not have their basis in the physical world; their basis lies in our mental world. I suggest that the information we can gather from looking inward is more accurate and more relevant concerning who we really are.

We change the state of our outer world by first changing the state of our inner world. Everything that comes to us must be processed through our collective consciousness. When we change that consciousness, we alter our perceptions and hence the world that we "see."

We soon come to the realization that in fact we are not who we think we are, for we have determined who we think we are from our past understanding of sensory inputs, all of which were arbitrary and open to many different interpretations. To have decided on only one interpretation at a certain point in time doesn't preclude us from making other choices at a later time, when we're more informed about our true nature. We are more—much, much more—than who we think we are, so much more that we'll never find out in our life-time.

There simply isn't enough time in 75 or so years of living to try all the things we need to try to find out all the things we can excel at. After all, it can take 10 to 15 years to become trained and knowledgeable in many of the professions, whether it be law, medicine or driving in the Indy 500. But there is time enough to find at least one major area, one particular area of excellence, and pursue and develop it into something both meaningful and significant.

This is the point: we must never lose sight of who we really are! WE ARE NOT WHO WE THINK WE ARE—although we always act out who we think we are in everything we say and do!

Each of us can decide what we will think about. We can focus on thoughts of our own choosing, rather than simply respond to the random stimuli from the outer world. We can resolve that the images in our mind will no longer primarily reflect the conditions in our environment, but rather our desired goals and aspirations. The immutable law is this: **only that which takes firm root in our consciousness has any impact and effect.** Therefore, if our inner vision

*Man is not the sum
of what he is
but the totality
of what he might be.*

ANONYMOUS

is fixed upon our desires, and we accept all sensory input only in this context, we are free from any possibility of defeat.

Managing Our Mental State

We know that the mind can concentrate on only one thought at a time. It is impossible to focus on two things simultaneously. So it's up to us to take time every day to ensure that we're thinking the right "thoughts" and picturing the right "pictures" that are consistent with the right "things"—who we want to be and where we want to go. If we keep our mind focused solely on our goal, the many distractions and frustrations in everyday life become mere minor irritants, rather than major roadblocks, along the way.

Here are five steps to manage and control your mental "state:"

1. Find a quiet place, and relax both your mind and body.
2. Repeat to yourself the new belief you wish to adopt that is consistent with the new behavior you want to have.
3. See yourself in your mind as already having the new belief and already performing in the desired way in as much detail as you can.
4. Bathe in the positive feelings this scene generates.
5. Mentally, add this new "experience" to your memory profile. Now you'll be able to recall it in an instant in order to relive the positive feelings.

This sequence involves three critical elements. You must

- affirm
- conceptualize, and
- emotionalize

the new belief, representing the idea component, the image component, and the emotional component—the three elements that comprise all new thought creation. To remember the sequence, simply think of the word "ace," or the letters A-C-E.

Every good thought
you think
is contributing its share
to the ultimate result
of your life.

GRENVILLE KLEISER
AMERICAN AUTHOR
(1868-1935)

This technique, which I call the A-C-E technique, allows us to purposely program our mind by imagining the things we want in as much detail as we can. We know we can creatively imagine an event in our mind in every detail and it automatically becomes part of our memory profile. By running our brain in this focused, purposeful way, we gain control over what we need the most—*the experience of success.* And we know that success, real or imagined, breeds success. So in order to have such experiences, we need only repeat them over and over again in our imagination.

Another way to gain control over our thoughts and actions is to see the positive in every event and circumstance in our life. Something positive can be found in even the most negative of events, if only we look long and hard. This may not be enough to outweigh all of the negative impact that is initially perceived. But such an approach at least gives balance and perspective to the inevitable ups and downs we all experience every day.

For example, if we're laid off from our job, we could spend all our time wallowing in self-pity and a sense of devastation. Or we could pull ourselves together, look at our options, and devise a plan to search for a new job that may both pay us more and challenge us more, and hence that would value us more. Easy? Of course not. But do we really have any choice if we want to move ahead?

Using such techniques, we can control our mental "state" instantly and 100 percent of the time. *For either we must shape our perceptions, or something or someone else will shape them for us.* Nothing has any meaning—until *we* give it some meaning. We know that if we change the idea of a thing, we change that thing. Likewise, when we change our impression of who we are—WE CHANGE WHO WE ARE!

Clearly, it is the quality of our inner communications that determines the quality of our outer lives. Our goal is to create optimum resourceful states that lead us to purposeful action rather than fearful retreat.

*The profoundest thought
or passion sleeps as in a mine,
until it is discovered
by an equal mind and heart.*

RALPH WALDO EMERSON
AMERICAN ESSAYIST,
PHILOSOPHER AND POET
(1803-1882)

The way to achieve this is to analyze and update our personal belief system, our self-image, and move it in the direction of our True Self. The process is

> **THINK**—What do I see/sense in my life?
>
> **RE-THINK**—Is this relevant? What does it mean?
>
> then . . . **THINK AGAIN**—What does it really mean in light of my True Self?

We are all born into a bondage of our senses, and as long as we place our trust in their validity, we remain slaves to them. As Teilhard de Chardin has observed, "We are not human beings having a spiritual experience; we are spiritual beings having a human experience." Our True Self is something that is indescribable. It is a power greater than any of us can ever hope to understand.

Focus on the Positives

You will recall Terry Anderson, a correspondent for The Associated Press who was finally released by his Lebanese captors in 1991. Despite nearly seven years of almost unbearable physical and emotional punishment, he not only survived his ordeal but looked surprisingly fit and healthy when he was released. How did he manage to do this? Could it be by controlling his thoughts?

Talking to the press, Anderson described the brutality of his confinement—the chains, blindfolds, rotten food and almost daily beatings by guards. "I was desperate to keep my brain alive," he told reporters. "I was deadly scared I would lapse into some kind of mental rot. What kept me going was my faith and my stubbornness. You wake up every day and summon up the energy."

Anderson could have fallen victim to his environment. There certainly were enough negative things going on around him such that if he had succumbed to them, they would have overwhelmed and

Man's capacities have never been measured; nor are we to judge of what he can do by any precedents, so little has been tried.

HENRY DAVID THOREAU
AMERICAN NATURALIST,
PHILOSOPHER AND WRITER
(1817-1862)

FIVE FABULOUS FACTS

1. Success is not an accident.

2. Success leaves clues; so does failure.

3. Success is the result of cause and effect.

4. Our thoughts are the cause, and our behavior and circumstances are the effect.

but

5. We can choose our thoughts, and hence control their effects.

As a result, we can all learn to become more successful . . . at anything!

*I know of no one
who has ever drowned
in his own sweat.*

ANONYMOUS

destroyed him. So he focused his thinking in another direction, on thoughts about himself and his future. He later explained that he thought about the fact he was still alive, that God and all his friends and family dearly loved and missed him. He thought about what he would do when he was free, how he would realign his priorities and spend his time. In the process, he was able to live a large part of his life in "another place," in a mental world of his own making. I wonder how many of us in his situation could have responded as well as he did.

We Think in Three Dimensions

In the last exercise, we described how we think in a three-dimensional format. Every thought we have has an "idea" component, an "image" component, and an "emotional" component. Consider the word "knife" as an example. The idea component that creates initial awareness is simply "knife." The image component is whatever picture we conjure up in our mind at the sound of the word. It is critical to understand that all the meaning lies in the image. For many, it may be a common table knife that we use while eating. The emotional component is then what we sense as a result of this image. It could be the fond memories from the past of eating dinner at Thanksgiving or Christmas at home with our families.

Others may imagine other kinds of knives, however. A doctor may see a sharp, surgical knife she uses to make an incision. This may give rise to feelings of healing and caring. A gourmet chef may imagine a cooking knife that he uses to prepare his favorite foods. He may have feelings of pride and appreciation, knowing his clients enjoy the fruits of his labor. Note that all the feelings we evoke are dependent on the particular image we conceive. If we were recently attacked on our way home by thugs wielding switch-blade knives, for example, our feelings about a knife may well be radically different. It's probably a topic of conversation we would prefer to avoid.

Self-image Psychology

This way that we think, in pictures and in three dimensions, is important in understanding what I call the THREE PILLARS OF THE SELF, which are

*What seems nasty, painful, evil,
can become a source of beauty,
joy and strength,
if faced with an open mind.
Every moment is a golden one
for him who has the vision
to recognize it as such.*

HENRY MILLER
AMERICAN WRITER
(1891-1980)

- the self-concept
- the self-image, and
- self-esteem.

An entirely new school of thought has arisen as a result of the discovery of the self-concept. The *self-concept* answers this question: **"Who do I think I am?"** It refers to the whole bundle of beliefs we have acquired that relate to our own sense of identity.

This brings us to what many consider to be the major psychological breakthrough of the 20th century, the understanding of the role of the self-image as it affects human behavior. It has come to be known as self-image psychology. Our *self-image* is the belief system we have adopted that answers this question: **"How do I 'see' myself . . . in the many facets of life?"**—what kind of mother, what kind of father, what kind of student, what kind of lover, what kind of worker? How well do I read, do I write, do I sing, do I dance, do I paint? How good am I at languages, at mathematics, at drawing, at mechanical repairs, at remembering names, at telling jokes?

It's important to note that educational researchers have discovered that a person's self-image is a more accurate predictor of performance than I.Q. In fact, our self-image determines our performance in every aspect of our life. We all know very talented people in music, sports or the arts who weren't able to develop their talent because of a poor self-image, while others with much less talent went on to successful careers because they were not inhibited by feelings of low self-esteem.

All this again proves the primary mental law: THOUGHT plus FAITH creates FORM. Our mind and nervous system work together in such a way that they bring into reality whatever pictures we accept and project onto our mental screen. The role of the Conscious Mind is always to produce the pictures. The role of the Subconscious Mind is always to ensure that all of our actions, feelings and behavior are consistent with these pictures, our self-image.

The Subconscious is always the obedient servant, the obliging

*Only in man's imagination
does every truth find an effective
and undeniable existence.
Imagination, not invention,
is the supreme master
of art, as of life.*

JOSEPH CONRAD
ENGLISH NOVELIST
(1857-1924)

slave to the conscious perception process. But once it has received its instructions, it becomes the most powerful influence in our life. It accepts all of our instructions without question, records them in every detail, and refers back to them on appropriate occasions. The Subconscious becomes intelligent unto itself in the exact way it has been programmed to think, and proceeds to bring into physical form whatever it has been programmed to do.

If we are ever victimized, it is by our Conscious Mind, not the Subconscious. *It is the conscious perception process that we rely upon to accurately reflect reality.* All failure can be traced back to the objective faculty of the mind—to our conscious thought processes.

Our self-image, then, is critical in two important ways. First, we always THINK AND ACT according to the dominant pictures we have in our head. The Subconscious Mind always acts on what our Conscious Mind has accepted as "true," on whatever we have decided consciously to believe or not believe.

As we have noted, most of us have more than one picture in our head that relates to any given activity, say public speaking. Some pictures depict us as succeeding at this activity, while others depict us as failing. Hence we get conflicting messages from our Subconscious, a little voice that one moment says, "Yes, this is FUN!" and the next moment says, "Hey, this is SCARY STUFF!" The thoughts that we allow to dominate our thinking at any particular time are the thoughts that will prevail. If we don't fix our thoughts consistently on one given set of pictures, on one particular outcome, our mind will simply flip back and forth. And we are confident one moment and terrified the next. I'm sure you'll agree, this is not the best way to deliver a great speech!

Second, our self-image determines what other people think of us, and hence how they respond and react. **Others usually see in us precisely what we see in ourselves.** By our words and actions, they gain an appreciation of our "sense of self"—who we think we are—and generally accept our opinion, having no other basis for comparison. They simply assume that we are in the best position to know the most about ourselves, when in fact often we are not.

*I have often thought that
the best way to define a man's character
would be to seek out the particular
mental and moral attitude in which,
when it came upon him,
he felt himself most deeply
and intensely active and alive.
At such moments there is a voice inside
which speaks and says,
"This is the real me!"*

WILLIAM JAMES
AMERICAN PSYCHOLOGIST
AND PHILOSOPHER
(1842-1910)

On occasion, others see in us things we don't see in ourselves. Their evaluation, based on evidence that they're able to see but we do not or cannot, leads them to disagree with our decision. This can cause them to decide that we think either too much or too little of ourselves, that we are either over-estimating or under-estimating our abilities. And often they try to convince us that we're wrong, but usually without success. We tend to value our opinions of ourselves over those of others. This is our enormous ego at work—WE THINK WE KNOW BEST! Of course, this view only keeps us locked into our current manner of thinking, and we stay exactly where we are.

The Concept of Layering

This leads us to a process I call "layering." We all look outward and see the world, with all its confusion and mixed messages. As well, we all look inward and see ourselves in the many facets of life—as a spouse, as a parent, as an employer, as an employee, as an athlete, as a cook, as a driver of a car, and on and on. Each of us has several thousand pictures stored in memory that depict how we see ourselves in various real-life situations.

In this way, we perceive and interpret things we see in the physical world around us in the context of how we see ourselves. This is "layering"—we lay on top of our pictures of the world the various pictures we already have of ourselves. For example, imagine that a salesperson is attempting to make you buy a product before you've made up your mind. You have several ways of responding: you could acquiesce, and give in; you could get mad, and leave; or you could simply state that you need more time to make your decision. How you respond to an over-zealous salesperson is largely a function of how you see yourself in such a situation: as passive, aggressive, or confident and assertive but still polite. The result is predictable: we always perform in our life according to the "pictures" we have of ourselves in our mind. Of course, this may or may not get us exactly what we want!

Thus when we change the pictures we have of ourselves, we change the way the world "looks" to us. It is our self-image—how we "see" ourselves—then, that determines the way we perceive, interpret and respond to all the things that come our way.

Live your life
so that whenever you lose,
you are ahead.

WILL ROGERS
AMERICAN HUMORIST AND ACTOR
(1879-1935)

If we want to bring about meaningful change in our life, our task is clear: *we must first change the state of our* **inner** *world if we want to change the state of our* **outer** *world.* This is the basis of self-image psychology. Everything begins with the PICTURES we have in our head that constitute our sense of self. Positive pictures allow us to take positive steps that lead to positive results. In this way, our mental pictures are transformed into their physical counterparts. And we get precisely what we want!

In his current best seller *The Seven Habits of Highly Effective People,* Dr. Steven R. Covey expands on and puts into a wider context much of what we have discussed in this chapter. He explains in detail what he calls the "inside-outside" approach to personal growth—that all meaningful change begins with our sense of who we think we are. As well, he explains how each of us can manage—in a conscious rather than unconscious way—the "gap" or small period of time between a given stimulus from our environment and our response to it to make better choices. I have benefited greatly from his insights, and highly recommend this book as one that deserves your serious attention.

*More than
any other thing,
we want
the conscious awareness
and
experience of worthiness.*

GERRY ROBERT
AUTHOR OF
CONQUERING LIFE'S CHALLENGES

YOU HAVE TO SET YOURSELF ON F-I-R-E!

IDA GUILLORY

Ida Guillory was born during the great depression on a farm in rural Louisiana. She was the fourth child of seven in a French-speaking sharecropper's family. The family was poor. The farm lacked all modern conveniences, including plumbing and electricity. But the family was rich in tradition. Her folks loved zydeco, the lively, accordion-based music still very popular in Louisiana today. And love for this music necessarily got into Ida's blood.

Later, in 1948, Ida's mother gave her three brothers a push-button accordion. She was trying to spark the boys' interest and love for the music. Ida was overlooked, since in those days it wasn't fashionable for girls to play such instruments. But none of the boys were interested. Eventually the accordion ended up in Ida's hands.

Now 65, she is Queen Ida, the reigning monarch of zydeco music. She has won a Grammy Award, released eight albums and introduced zydeco music to audiences around the world. And she hasn't stopped here. Her success at playing the folk music of Louisiana's Creole population has prompted her to author a cookbook featuring her favorite recipes for spicy Cajun dishes like gumbo, jambalaya and étoufée. Today Ida is enjoying life to the fullest, and enriching others' lives in the process.

You make a difference by giving something of yourself for the betterment of others. Ida Guillory has made a difference. She dared to dream big dreams, and in the process, she set herself on fire!

*The world
marvels and makes way
for those who know
what they want,
and have the courage
to actively pursue it.*

WALTER STAPLES

CHAPTER 5

Self-esteem Is Everything

You have no idea what a poor opinion I have of myself
—and how little I deserve it!
—W. S. Gilbert

How Much Do I Like Myself?

We now come to *self-esteem,* and the importance of self-love. Self-esteem is the emotional component of the self-concept and represents the real core of human personality. It is generally agreed by psychologists that self-esteem is the most critical element affecting all human performance. It answers this question: **"How do I FEEL about myself—how much do I like, respect and value myself . . . in the way I now see myself?"** Our self-image may be high or it may be low, it may be consistent or inconsistent with reality, but our self-esteem is always

TRUE TO THE PICTURES WE HOLD IN OUR MIND.

In other words, the PICTURES that collectively represent our self-image are at the root of how much we like ourselves. So if we want to change how much we like ourselves, we have to change how we "see" ourselves—the PICTURES we have in our head. More positive pictures produce more positive self-liking.

Thus how much we like ourselves is totally dependent on who we think we are—our conception of ourselves. It is either our inner catalyst or our inner brake. It either propels us forward or it holds us back. It is the most important single statement we can make about ourselves as a person.

So we see that of the three pillars of the self, the image component of our self-concept is the most critical, since it is the component over which we can exercise the most control. The feeling component, that collectively determines our self-esteem, is AUTOMATIC. It is totally dependent on all the pictures we have accepted as representing who we think we are.

*The truth is that, like every
other part of nature, human beings
have an internal imperative to grow.
With enough sun and water to put down
deep roots of self-esteem, children
can withstand terrible storms. Without them,
the slightest wind will seem full of danger.*

GLORIA STEINEM
FROM *REVOLUTION FROM WITHIN*

The importance of self-esteem is seen from the following comments by Dorothy Corkille Briggs in her insightful book *Your Child's Self-Esteem.*

> What is self-esteem? It is how a person feels about himself. It is his overall judgment of himself—how he likes his person. A person's judgment of self influences the kinds of friends he chooses, how he gets along with others, the kind of person he marries, and how productive he will be. It affects his creativity, integrity, stability, and even whether he will be a leader or follower. His feelings of self-worth form the core of his personality and determine the use he makes of his aptitudes and abilities. His attitude toward himself has a direct bearing on how he lives all parts of his life. In fact, self-esteem is the mainspring that slates each of us for success or failure as a human being.

Here are some recent statistics: almost 10 percent of all teenagers try to commit suicide (they opt for a very permanent solution to a very temporary problem); one in 10 teenage girls gets pregnant each year; 50 percent of high school seniors get drunk at least once a month; and 1 in 5 young people verge on being obese.

The deepest human need is for self-respect, self-worth and self-liking—it's all tied into our self-concept, our sense of personal identity. Without high self-esteem, we certainly can't perform at our optimum. In fact, many of us begin to self-destruct—break down physically, mentally and spiritually—when we don't feel good about ourselves and lack meaning in our life. It follows that anything we can do to make ourselves feel more important, more worthy and more capable directly increases our self-esteem.

The Power of Negative Thinking

In terms of our general health and overall mental state, we must understand that emotions of any kind have a dramatic effect on our body and central nervous system. We know that negative emotions follow from negative thoughts, and positive emotions follow from positive thoughts. Clearly we have to control our thoughts if we want to control our feelings. Why? Because in many cases, these feelings

Guilt is never a rational thing;
it distorts all the faculties
of the human mind,
it perverts them,
it leaves a man no longer in
the free use of his reason,
it puts him into confusion.

EDMUND BURKE
ENGLISH STATESMAN AND ORATOR
(1729-1797)

can KILL US! In fact, every day people are dying of boredom, despair, worry, fear, hatred, anger, guilt, resentment . . . and so on. A great book came out in 1988 titled *You Can't Afford the Luxury of a Negative Thought*. And you can't. The price is simply too high.

Charles W. Mayo, founder of the Mayo Clinic, once commented, "Worry affects the circulation, the heart, the glands, the whole nervous system, and profoundly affects health. I have never known a person who died from overwork, but many who died from doubt."

What do negative emotions tell us? **All negative emotions tell us that we're not running our brain very effectively!** We're allowing ourselves to focus excessively on negative thoughts. And we're certainly NOT going to get the results we want when we're locked into an UN-resourceful state. Consider the effects of the following negative emotions:

fear: We want to be UN-fearful of something, yet we cannot when we're immobilized and often terrorized by fear.

anger: We want others to change their behavior, yet they cannot when we use anger as a confrontational tool (everything looks like a nail when your only tool is a hammer!).

anxiety: We want to cope more effectively with a given situation, yet we cannot because we're rendered powerless by the effects of stressful thoughts.

guilt: We want to forgive ourselves and move on with our lives, but we cannot because we're obsessed with wanting to punish ourselves, or so it seems, over and over again.

For example, consider the effects on the human body that anger is able to precipitate. A study published in the August 1992 issue of *The American Journal of Cardiology* is the first to document a change in heart function brought on by anger. Its conclusion: the things that make our blood boil are damaging to our heart! This finding, that the heart's pumping efficiency is reduced by between five and seven percent and more when people get mad, adds to the growing body

*ℜothing can
work me damage
except myself.
The harm that I sustain
I carry about with me,
and am never a real sufferer
but by my own fault.*

SAINT BERNARD
FOUNDER OF THE CISTERCIAN ORDER
(1091-1153)

of evidence that indicates anger-prone individuals are far more likely to develop severe heart disease, and earlier in life, than those who are not. Dr. Peter Kaufman, acting chief of the Behavioral Medicine Branch of the National Heart, Lung and Blood Institute said, "A finding . . . that demonstrates a direct effect on heart function from anger, is important. It underscores the role of emotions like anger in the development of heart disease."

Negative emotions contribute to poor health in many ways. People who are stressful, angry or unhappy are generally over-fatigued and don't look after themselves very well. They don't eat, sleep or exercise properly. These same feelings often contribute to high blood pressure, putting at risk key organs and the whole cardiovascular system. As well, negative emotions suppress our immune system, causing ailments as simple as arthritis and the common cold to more serious ones that can include pneumonia and cancer. The message is simple enough: we need to control our emotions if we want to be happy and productive people. Also if we want to live longer!

It's interesting to wonder why human beings were given feelings at all. For if we were simple robots, we wouldn't experience any pain or pleasure. My theory supports the notion of a grand design behind all things. It hypothesizes that our Maker gave feelings to man to ensure that a moral dimension to human behavior would evolve naturally. After all, as we have just seen, those who practice evil versus good and anger versus love tend not to live very long due to the negative physical effects of this type of behavior. Hence over the long term, their kind will not generate as many offspring as others who are more positive-minded. Although none of us will live long enough to see if this theory in fact has any merit, we know even in the short term that positive feelings are worthwhile, that they simply make life more interesting and more productive, and a lot more fun!

Low self-esteem is believed to be at the root of practically every human affliction and all unproductive behavior. Everything from anger, rudeness, timidness, arrogance, over-indulgence, greed, self-pity, selfishness, aggressiveness, depression and suicide are prime examples. Dr. Nathanial Branden, a clinical psychologist and author of

*Don't
find fault—
find a
remedy.*

HENRY FORD
AMERICAN INDUSTRIALIST
(1863-1947)

nine books on self-esteem, wrote, "I cannot think of a single psychological problem that is not traceable to a poor self-concept. Positive self-esteem is a cardinal requirement of a fulfilling life."

Other examples of negative behavior brought on by low self-esteem include:

Blaming and complaining: People who blame others and complain about their circumstances refuse to accept the fact that they are responsible for everything that happens to them in their life. It is always so much easier to blame people or things "out there" than to say, "It's me who has the problem; it's me who has to change. I am responsible." The person who habitually blames and complains feels insecure and inadequate, and doesn't have the self-esteem to deal effectively with the real problems in his or her life.

Need for constant attention and approval: People who have a need for constant attention and approval are unable to recognize and appreciate themselves as worthy and deserving. They have a compulsive need for continuous confirmation and reinforcement that they are "OK," that they are acceptable in the eyes of others.

Need to always be right: People who suffer from low self-esteem are always trying to compensate for their feelings of inadequacy by proving that they are right and others are wrong. It's a classic case of not wanting to show any weakness or lack of ability.

Fear of failure and fear of rejection: These two fears hold more people back from achieving their full potential than any other aspect of human personality. Such fears prevent people from taking action in areas that are new or risky; hence they have no goals and are not motivated to act in any purposeful way. Such people simply lack the self-image and self-esteem to overcome the negative feelings that failure and rejection bring on.

A Lesson for Charlie Brown

I often talk to people who are hurting inside—to students and parents, the unemployed and disillusioned—about how to begin to feel better about themselves. Here's a summary of what I tell them. My title is—IN SEARCH OF HAPPINESS.

*Regret
for the things we did
can be tempered by time;
it is regret for the things
we did not do
that is inconsolable.*

SYDNEY J. HARRIS
AMERICAN JOURNALIST AND AUTHOR
(1917-1986)

What is the one thing everyone in this world wants? The answer: everyone wants to be happy, to feel good about himself or herself, to feel important, wanted, to be RELEVANT.

So how do we achieve this? To feel important, to feel relevant follows from DOING something, something that we believe is significant. It could be music, writing, dancing, athletic or scholastic pursuits, being a homemaker, raising children, being a plumber, a teacher, a student, a farmer, a businessperson—to be an achiever of some kind at something we think is important.

In every group and organization, there are both high achievers and low achievers. This is an interesting fact because we all have, as an inherent trait, the desire to achieve. Indeed, Abraham Maslow is famous for describing these needs in his hierarchy of human wants and needs. In other words, our Creator endowed us with this characteristic as a birthright. He wanted us to aim higher, He wanted us to stretch, to be more, do more and have more. He wanted each of us TO WANT TO contribute to society something that was meaningful and consistent with who we really are.

Clearly, wanting to achieve or not to achieve is not in question. What, then, allows some people to achieve at a higher level than others? The behavioral answer is: high achievers are those who are capable of taking purposeful action toward whatever goal is being sought, whereas low achievers are those who are not capable of taking such action. This doesn't have to involve something exotic like exploring the Amazon or climbing Mount Everest. It could involve taking daily walks, preparing a hearty meal, meeting some new people, joining a fitness club or a charity, helping a fundraising event, taking night courses or applying for a new job. The goal itself is not important. What is important is that the activity you undertake makes you FEEL BETTER! That's all.

So what allows some people to take action, while others cannot? The answer, of course, is self-esteem. Some people have it, and it acts as a catalyst; a great many people do not, and it acts as a brake.

*Don't go around saying
the world owes you a living;
the world owes you nothing—
it was here first.*

MARK TWAIN
AMERICAN NOVELIST AND HUMORIST
(1835-1910)

The obvious question now is, "Why is it that some people have high self-esteem and others do not?" The reality is that most people look to the world around them to establish their level of self-esteem. They expect their friends, their neighbors, their employer, their spouse, their children—anyone and everyone—to GIVE IT TO THEM. And when this doesn't happen, they claim that other people HAVE CAUSED THEM to have low self-esteem.

Good grief, Charlie Brown! Such people are looking in the wrong place. They need to realize that the world at large is not in the business of trying to make them happy. The world is too busy doing other things! It doesn't have the ability to take "time out" to deal specifically with each and every one of us in the precise way we would like. How can anyone logically believe that the world has the RESPONSIBILITY to make everyone in it happy?

At best, the world sends us mixed messages. The news on the radio, TV, movies and newspapers all too often focus on famines, natural disasters, war, disease, poverty and death—all negative. And on occasion they focus on a birth, a wedding, a new home, loving relationships, caring friends, the sun, green grass and clear water—all positive. There is no rhyme or reason or consistency in this chaotic and unpredictable world. Simply to hope to find positive things in our environment on a regular basis is to decide to surrender our well-being to CHANCE, to forces outside our control. I suggest that relying on chance to get you where you want to go is not a very wise bet to make.

An interesting book came out recently with a great title, *What You Think Of Me Is None Of My Business*. And it really isn't. Who cares what other people think of you? You can never hope to have everyone in this world like you. It's just not possible. Their opinions are simply "opinions," and you shouldn't let these be the main basis for deciding who YOU THINK you are.

Another problem we must be aware of is that we often misinterpret messages from the world around us based on our already low

*What the inner voice
says will not disappoint
the hoping soul.*

JOHANN VON SCHILLER
GERMAN POET AND DRAMATIST
(1759-1805)

opinion of ourselves. We make preconceived judgments on every-day events and happenings, and thus color them to make them consistent with our current fixed beliefs. A person can say something quite innocent or even positive about us—yet we twist the comment in our minds, reading into it something cynical or negative that was not really intended.

Where, then, can you turn to decide WHO YOU REALLY ARE? The answer is clear: **you ask YOURSELF!** YOU decide. You reach down into the very center of your soul and find the answer. And when you do, you'll find that you really do believe you are worthy, you are capable, you are productive, you are loved—you are RELEVANT! You know it in your heart! You just KNOW IT! I know it about me. You know it about you. Why is this? I don't know. But whoever made us . . . MADE US THIS WAY!

Don't deny your worth. Don't DE-value yourself. Don't argue with the still small voice within. Just accept the TRUTH—and get on with living, with giving, with being who you really are, despite anything the world is telling you. The fact is—the world is waiting to hear from you. It is waiting for you to say who you are. It is waiting for you to decide—because that was the way you were created. You were given the responsibility to CHOOSE.

Just think how fantastic this fact is. You have the final say, the ability to crown your life with dignity and self-respect . . . with GLORY. You owe it to yourself, and you owe it to me and the world at large to share the fruits of your greatness. If you can see what a great challenge this is, what a great opportunity—then you'll be excited about life forever! And this is the way it was meant to be!

Having read the above, imagine overhearing this conversation between Lucy and Charlie Brown.

Lucy: "Charlie Brown, you're always putting yourself down. You think you can't do anything well. What is your problem?"

*The more a person feels he
has control over his future,
the more responsibility he will
accept for all of his actions.*

WALTER STAPLES

Charlie Brown: "I don't know anyone who would believe me if I said otherwise. Who would I be kidding?"

Lucy: "Charlie Brown, you are the one who has to believe. Why don't you ask yourself?"

Charlie Brown: "Are you INSANE? How am I supposed to know?"

Obviously, Charlie Brown hasn't read my article!

Turning Our Life Around

If we were to summarize on a chart the positive and negative effects of low and high self-esteem, it would look something like this:

effects of low self-esteem	*effects of high self-esteem*
no goals/no direction	specific goals/clear direction
failing relationships	meaningful relationships
lack of self-confidence	lots of self-confidence
low personal productivity	high personal productivity
avoids responsibility	accepts responsibility
low energy level	high energy level
undisciplined	disciplined
unproductive behavior— fear, anger, guilt, jealousy, depression, risk-avoider	productive behavior— friendly, forgiving, accepting, supportive, risk-taker

Clearly, our level of self-esteem is the controlling element that affects the way we perform in every aspect of our life.

Consider the following 12 questions—what I call the "dirty dozen" —that may give you some insight into your own level of self-esteem. They all won't apply to everyone but see if a few might apply to you:

*Let us be thankful
for the fools;
but for them
the rest of us
could not succeed.*

MARK TWAIN
AMERICAN NOVELIST AND HUMORIST
(1835-1910)

1. Why do I eat so much (or so little)?
2. Why do I exercise so little (or so much)? . . . Charles Atlas was a 98 lb weakling in his teens.
3. Why do I drink alcohol so much (or at all)?
4. Why do I shout at my family so much (or ignore them)?
5. Why do I sleep so much (or so little)?
6. Why do I watch television so much (or at all)?
7. Why do I dislike my job so much (or working, period)?
8. Why do I avoid making new friends (or meeting new people, period)?
9. Why do I never finish what I start (or never start anything)?
10. Why do I think I can't accomplish anything significant?
11. Why do I think others are worthy of success, but I'm not?
12. Why do I find life so boring (or is it I who is boring)?

Think what higher self-esteem and greater self-confidence could do for you in your own particular career, whatever line of work you are in. If you are active in sales of one kind or another, for example, consider these 10 significant benefits:

- more effective use of the telephone
  - better at cold-calling
- more dynamic sales presentations
  - better at handling difficult customers
- better at handling rejection
  - better at setting and reaching goals
- better at closing sales
  - more productive relationships
- lower stress and anxiety, and hence
  - better able to provide a valuable service to people who want and truly need it

Now consider how improved performance in all these areas could translate into increased earnings . . . weekly, monthly, yearly and over a whole career. What does an extra $100 a week mean? It means an extra $5,000 a year, or over $1 million when compounded over a 35-year period!

Here are some suggestions you may want to consider to bring about significant change in your life:

*The difference between
playing to win
and playing not to lose
is the difference between
success and mediocrity.*

ANONYMOUS

1. Forgive anyone and everyone who has ever done you any harm at any time in your life, including YOURSELF. Forgiving yourself may well be the hardest thing of all. Through the process of forgiving, you'll be clearing your mind and body of all toxic influences, thereby letting you move on with your life. I like this advice from Oscar Wilde, the Irish poet and dramatist: "Always forgive your enemies. Nothing annoys them so much."

2. As of today, stop blaming any external factors or other people for your current state of affairs. You can't keep focusing on the outside when all meaningful change and improvement must begin from the inside. And understand that the world can't change you for the better, even if it wanted to. Only you can do that.

3. Accept the notion that you and only you are in charge of your circumstances, that you and only you are responsible for what happens to you in your life. Take the approach, "My future is in my hands. I am responsible. I accept the challenge!"

4. Adopt the belief that all the things that have ever happened to you in your life up to now—both good and bad—have happened for a reason and a purpose, and will serve you in the future. Accept what has happened, learn from the experience, and move on. The alternative is to stay exactly where you are!

5. And remember—results don't lie. Look at the results you're now getting in your life. Are you happy with these results? Do you want to change these results? How badly do you want to change them? If you want to change, are you prepared to make a firm commitment, and resolve to do what you know needs to be done?

Learning from Our Mistakes

We come now to the role that FAILURE has played in the evolution of mankind. The species of man wandering around our planet today had a hard time getting here. We all descended from homo sapiens who survived and won out over other species who perished. Let's consider some of the challenges faced by prehistoric man in his everyday life:

*Only the curious will learn
and only the resolute overcome
the obstacles to learning.
The quest quotient has
always excited me more than
the intelligence quotient.*

EUGENE S. WILSON
AMERICAN EDUCATOR AND AUTHOR
(1905-1981)

famine and disease
climatic upheavals
marauding tribes
wild animals

So while others failed, we evolved by

- **adapting** (furs for clothing; caves for shelter and protection);
- **innovating** (bones and rocks for utensils and weapons);
- **experimenting** (fire; growing and eating different foods); and
- **communicating** (using pictures and hand signals to communicate. There was survival in numbers if you could persuade others to join you).

It was the group that did these and other things that overcame obstacles and survived. Its members through trial and error discovered and put into practice what I call a Natural Success Formula that exists to this day:

1. Decide what you want.
2. Take action.
3. Assess your results (decide what worked, what didn't).
4. Change your approach.
5. Keep on taking action . . . all the while focusing on the desired outcome.

Consider what steps you and I took NATURALLY when we were very young and wanted to walk, talk, eat, dress, read, write or ride a bicycle. By the age of five, we were doing many or all of these things. But did anyone have to teach us these five steps of the learning process? Of course not. We knew them INSTINCTIVELY because they are part of our heritage, part of our prehistoric past. From this process, we see an obvious fact of life: **failure is a vital and necessary**

*Success
is always found
at the end of a long road
strewn with the debris
of numerous failures.*

WALTER STAPLES

part of the achievement process. For it is by learning from our mistakes that we eventually succeed at whatever it is we want to do well.

So there is a Natural Success Formula that we have come to know through the evolution of our species. It is an unconscious knowledge fully ingrained as a survival instinct. Why is it then that when we're older, we STOP using this formula that worked so well for us in our youth? Could it be because of

- fear of failure (I can't handle the PAIN associated with more failure)?
- fear of success (any success I might achieve in this area would not be consistent with the way I now SEE MYSELF)?
- a subconscious desire to punish ourselves for not living up to our full potential (I don't believe I DESERVE to do well)?

It all comes back to low self-esteem—we don't *VALUE* ourselves enough—and the pleasure-pain principle: all our behavior is directed at either gaining pleasure or avoiding pain. If, in the pursuit of pleasure, however, we perceive there is a higher probability of pain (the fear of failure, rejection or embarrassment), we'll retreat back to where pleasure-pain are balanced off. In other words, there is no great pleasure there but at the same time, there is no great pain either. We all tend to stay in the relative comfort of our comfort zone.

There is a great contradiction in the term "grown up" because when we have grown up, we often become less proficient at LEARNING new things, at WANTING new things, and at DOING new things. OPTION? The only option we have is to do in a conscious way what was an unconscious process to growth and self-fulfillment as a child. And to be able to do this, we must work diligently on our sense of self, our answer to the first of the Ultimate Questions, "Who am I?" Specifically, we must find ways to dramatically increase our sense of self-worth: how much we value and "esteem" ourselves.

*The superior man
thinks
always of virtue;
the common man
thinks
only of comfort.*

CONFUCIUS
CHINESE PHILOSOPHER AND TEACHER
(557-479 B.C.)

YOU HAVE TO SET YOURSELF ON F-I-R-E!

MARK HUGHES

Tragedy paid a visit to Mark's home in Los Angeles when he was only 18 years old. And it was to change the course of the rest of his life.

The story began a few years earlier. After having her children, Mark's mom found herself about 35 pounds overweight. And she was determined to lose this weight to regain her former figure. His mom sought help from her doctor who prescribed various pills that were supposed to have the desired effect. Unfortunately, the pills also made her extremely hyper and unable to sleep. To counter this, her doctor recommended sleeping pills. She soon became addicted to a daily routine of these uppers and downers. And at the age of only 36, she died.

Soon afterwards, Mark moved in with his grandparents. After completing grade 9, he quit school. Because of his mother's problems, he had developed a keen interest in diet and nutrition, but knew virtually nothing about the subject. He began by working for various companies specializing in this field, but felt that their products were questionable and ineffective. So he began a serious study on his own of the whole health food industry. Soon he discovered various high quality food products that NASA had developed for their astronauts associated with the Apollo space program. At the same time, he became an expert in herbal medicine that has been used in China for thousands of years.

With this knowledge firmly in hand, Mark founded Herbalife International in Los Angeles in 1980, a firm that specializes in the very products he wishes were available to his mom when she needed them. In his first year, sales totalled $2 million. Today, the company has more than 500,000 distributors active in over 25 countries around the world, and sales of about $1 billion.

You make a difference by giving something of yourself for the betterment of others. Mark Hughes has made a difference. He dared to dream big dreams, and in the process, he set himself on fire!

*How many cares
one loses when one decides
not to be something, but
to be someone.*

COCO GABRIELLE CHANEL

CHAPTER 6

The Comfort Zone Complex

> There are days I just feel like crawling back
> into the womb—anyone's will do!
> —Woody Allen

Finding a Place to Hide

Let's explore what I call the comfort zone complex.

We all live in an area known as our comfort zone. Its parameters are totally defined by our self-image and level of self-esteem. Our comfort zone is our safe haven—it's our security zone. It's why we keep doing the same things the same way over and over again. Our comfort zone dictates that we avoid all risk that is above what our current self-image is able to support. So what do we do? We retreat, and do what is safe and non-threatening. We engage in what is known as habitual behavior. Such behavior is evident in our everyday habits—how we fold our arms, cross our legs, the food we eat, the friends we have, the books we read, the challenges we accept—everything we do in our life.

Test yourself. Fold your arms. Some people do it one way, others the other. Whatever way you do it, you are used to doing it the way that is most comfortable for you. OK, now undo your arms and fold them the other way. Do you find this way considerably more UN-comfortable? Try the same thing by crossing your legs the usual way, then the other way. Same sensation?

The comfort zone represents all the things we have done often enough to feel comfortable doing them again. Whenever we try something new, it falls outside the limits of our comfort zone. In this area, we feel fear, anxiety, apprehension—symptoms of "unworthiness"—all the undesirable feelings we generally associate with being "uncomfortable." When we anticipate feeling uncomfortable about doing something, we usually succumb to the fear and forgo the thought. We simply return to thoughts, feelings and actions that are more acceptable, more . . . well, more comfortable!

*Courage is doing
what you're afraid to do.
There can be no courage
unless you're scared.*

EDDIE RICKENBACKER
AMERICAN AVIATOR
(1890-1973)

The concept that "we shouldn't try new things" came from our childhood protectors—parents, teachers, adults, and other well-wishers of all kinds. They often used fear as a tool to ensure our physical well-being: "Don't touch that hot stove; don't play in the street; don't talk to strangers." And their warnings succeeded in most cases in getting us safe and sound to where we are today. So this approach—instilling fear of trying new things—has served a certain purpose. A problem always arises later in life, however, when we cling to our old ways, despite the fact that as adults we are much better equipped to tell the difference between what is dangerous and what is not.

If we want to change and try something new, we have to accept being uncomfortable, sometimes very uncomfortable, for a while. Then—surprise!—after repeated effort, uncomfortable becomes comfortable. And in the process, we expand our comfort zone. You will experience this yourself by repeatedly folding your arms or crossing your legs in the more uncomfortable way over a certain period of time, usually at least 21 days.

Most of us are comfortable with the prospect of a significant success where the probability of failure is minimal. For example, betting $1 on a lottery ticket where the prize is $1 million is an everyday occurrence. At the same time, most of us are uncomfortable with the prospect of a major failure. No one would buy a lottery ticket if all the losers were to be lined up and shot the very next morning! Playing the lottery may not be the best example to understand basic human motivations that lie behind real-life choices people make. Nevertheless, regarding the achievement process where the prospect of significant success is offset by the prospect of significant failure, we find that a general rule applies: we can hope to be successful in a big way only if we're also comfortable with the prospect of failing in a big way.

The following performance charts attempt to show graphically what we have just discussed.

FIGURE 2. A negative self-image produces low self-esteem that results in low achievement.

Every human being on this earth is born with a tragedy, and it isn't original sin. He's born with the tragedy that he has to grow up. A lot of people don't have the courage to do it.

HELEN HAYES
AMERICAN ACTRESS
(1900-1993)

In this mode, our self-image is weak and contracting, in turn narrowing the size of our comfort zone—where pleasure-pain are balanced off. We are more uncertain, more fearful and more protective of ourselves. We are comfortable only at being comfortable, hovering just above and below zero on the performance chart, the so-called "dead-zone" on a thermometer. As our self-image continues to decrease, it forces the upper and lower limits of our comfort zone to converge even more toward zero, and things get even worse. We become what is called **"dysfunctional"** and, like a recluse, we seek out ways to hide from the world.

FIGURE 3. A positive self-image produces high self-esteem that results in high achievement.

In this mode, our self-image is strong and expanding, in turn widening the size of our comfort zone—where pleasure-pain are balanced off. We are more confident, more assertive and more venturesome—we are able to test our outer limits. At our very best, we are what is called a **"free-flowing, fully functional"** personality. Fear of success on the upper end of the performance chart and fear of failure on the lower end mean nothing to such a person. They just fall away like water off a duck. But the same fears immobilize a person with a negative self-image. It's as though that person becomes cast in concrete, unable to move. All of us, whether we have a strong self-image or a weak self-image, suffer to some extent from the comfort zone complex, because in practical terms, our self-image will never equate to our True Self.

*In the heating
and air conditioning trade,
the point on the thermostat
in which neither heating nor
cooling must operate
—around 72 degrees—
is called
"The Comfort Zone."
It's also known as
"The Dead Zone."*

RUSSEL BISHOP

THE COMFORT ZONE COMPLEX

FIGURE 2

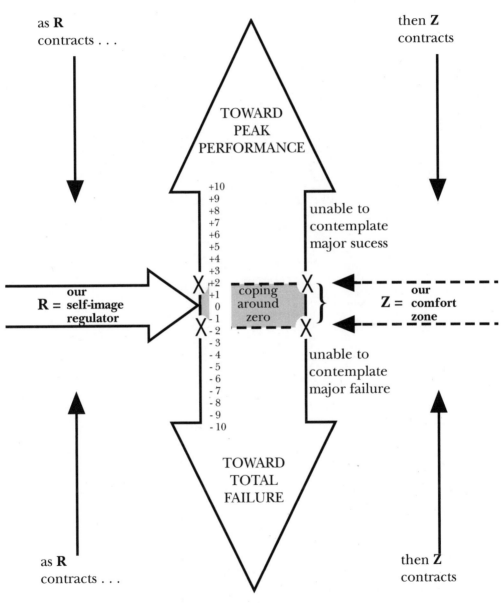

as **R**
contracts . . .

then **Z**
contracts

TOWARD
PEAK
PERFORMANCE

+10
+9
+8
+7
+6
+5
+4
+3
+2
+1
0
-1
-2
-3
-4
-5
-6
-7
-8
-9
-10

unable to
contemplate
major sucess

R = **our
self-image
regulator**

coping
around
zero

Z = **our
comfort
zone**

unable to
contemplate
major failure

TOWARD
TOTAL
FAILURE

as **R**
contracts . . .

then **Z**
contracts

If we want to escape from a prison,
we first have to realize that we're in one.
—Walter Staples

*You have to leave
the city of your comfort
and go into the wilderness
of your intuition.
What you'll discover
will be wonderful.
What you'll discover
will be yourself.*

ALAN ALDA
AMERICAN ACTOR

THE COMFORT ZONE COMPLEX

FIGURE 3

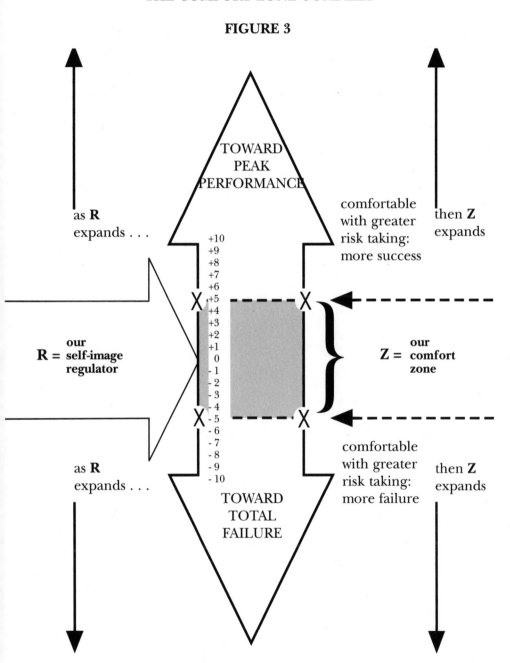

N.B. The term "comfort zone" was first used to describe human behavior in 1961 by James Newman, author of *Release Your Brakes!*

*Things turn out best
for the people who make the best
of the way things turn out.*

JOHN WOODEN
FORMER UCLA BASKETBALL COACH

Breaking Out of a Prison of Our Own Making

Our objective is always to expand our self-image, and hence the area of the possible by significantly widening the size of our comfort zone. Specifically, we want the boundaries to move both higher and lower on the performance chart. We want to be able to take greater risk on the one hand, and be comfortable with the prospect of success, all the while wanting to be able to accept the possibility of great defeat on the other, and be comfortable with the prospect of failure. We have to test our outer limits if we want to explore the extent of our full potential.

We know that discomfort is a fact of life for anyone wanting more. Yet we must learn to live with it, accept it—we must even seek it out. For discomfort is a sure sign of growth, of wanting to improve ourselves and our situation in life.

Have you heard the story of Sylvester Stallone, the actor who spent several years trying to break into the entertainment business, and found only rejection and ridicule everywhere he went? Casting directors in all the major studios thought he looked rather dumb and couldn't talk properly. Well, maybe! One night, he got an idea. He had just watched Chuck Wepner go the distance with heavyweight champion Mohammed Ali, and was very impressed how the crowd cheered on the underdog. Deeply inspired, he sat down and for three days and three nights, wrote the script for the movie Rocky.

The *Rocky* series, which numbers five to date, has grossed hundreds of millions of dollars worldwide, not to mention the fact that the name "Rocky" (and later "Rambo") has become a household name around the world. Here's a comment he made during an interview about what he thought people had to do if they wanted to become successful: "If you want something badly enough, you have to—eat lightning and crap thunder!" Now, I'm sure you'll agree, that's willing to be more than just a little uncomfortable!

Mastery Over Life

Many people spend their whole life rather like unseeing robots, reacting more often than acting in response to outside stimuli. They operate as predictable equations going through the motions according to a limited understanding of who they really are. Few ever

*We look at it
and do not see it;
Its name is The Invisible.
We listen to it
and do not hear it;
Its name is The Inaudible.
We touch it
and do not find it;
Its name is The Formless.*

LAO-TZU
CHINESE PHILOSOPHER,
MORALIST AND FOUNDER OF TAOISM
(604-531 B.C.)

face up to the primary challenges of life: expanding their inner consciousness, discovering their True Self, developing their full potential.

Mastery over life cannot be achieved through domination over our physical world. It comes through an understanding of the inner workings of our mind. As enlightened practitioners, we should not attempt to force the world to do our bidding. Rather we should strive to expand our collective consciousness to allow us to see the world according to our basic beliefs and aspirations. We should work and act in harmony with events and circumstances, rather than try to control and shape them. This way we're better able to cope with difficult and trying times, knowing that the dominant thoughts in our mind will eventually be manifested in our life. By letting go, we begin to see the things we need to see and do the things we need to do in order to bring us closer to our stated goals and objectives. We know that to change our outer world, we must first change our inner world. We never see the world as it really is. We always see it in the context of how we see ourselves.

Our collective consciousness defines who we are. It lies at the very center of our sense of self. Our mere state of being alive adds nothing to our understanding of who we really are. Our consciousness initially learns of itself through repeated reaction to stimuli from our environment. In this, it has no choice. This necessarily moulds us into thinking we're something we're not. For the random stimuli of the physical world know nothing of our True Self.

But we can question and resist messages from the physical world around us. We can envision even the exact opposite, thus conditioning our mind to adopt a view more in accordance with what we want rather than with what we don't want. We can cast up—AT WILL—mental pictures in our mind. Imagination is the magic tool by which we can become FREE—free from the bondage of our physical senses that can perceive only a physical world.

Our consciousness always functions in accordance with its limited knowledge of itself. It is constantly learning and constantly changing, yet is never complete. It is forever seeking to know itself better. This

When you grow in consciousness
and begin to see
the exciting world around you
in new and different ways,
you begin to get a larger vision
of yourself and what you think
you can accomplish in your life.

WALTER STAPLES

it can do through introspection and contemplation as practiced during meditation. And when such knowledge grows and expands beyond previous limits, a whole new world appears before our very eyes—we have new thoughts, we see new things, we experience new feelings. Everything has a new meaning. The things we see now were certainly there before, only before our limited consciousness was not able to "see" them. In this way, we move toward a new self, a more empowered self—toward our True Self.

The Quantum Leap Concept

We now come to the Quantum Leap concept. This concept says that incremental improvement can only lead to incremental change, that to bring about significant change in performance and results, we must avoid traditional methodologies that we have used before and are comfortable with. Quantum leaps result when we believe there is a better, much more efficient way to do something.

Think back in history and recall some discoveries, representing quantum leaps, that revolutionized various aspects of our world:

• gunpowder revolutionized warfare

Someone believed there was a more powerful way to project an object through the air than using a bow and arrow or throwing a stone.

• the internal combustion engine revolutionized transportation

Someone believed there was a more powerful way to propel a vehicle than simply tying more horses together.

• the assembly line revolutionized manufacturing

Someone believed there was a more efficient way to build things than doing them one at a time.

$\mathfrak{I}$ *can say,*
"I am terribly frightened
and fear is terrible and awful and
it makes me uncomfortable, so I
won't do that because it's uncomfortable."
Or I could say,
"Get used to being uncomfortable.
It is uncomfortable
doing something that's risky."
But so what?
Do you want to stagnate
and just be comfortable?

BARBRA STREISAND
POPULAR AMERICAN SINGER

- the transistor revolutionized electronics

Someone believed there was a more effective way to harness the flow of electrons than using copper wire.

- Morse code revolutionized communications

Someone believed there was a more reliable way to send messages than using smoke signals or beating on a drum.

Most people operate with the mindset that says success can come only one step at a time. The notion is that gradual progress will result from an incremental increase in effort. But this is the safe approach. Because if you do only a little more of what you're already doing, you'll only get a little more of what you've already got. And this doesn't make for a quantum leap.

And simply trying harder and harder can result in less and less—you quickly reach a point of diminishing returns. If you want to make a quantum leap, more effort is seldom the answer. A prime example is speed-reading. Studies have found that the average adult in America reads at the 7th or 8th grade level. But even many university graduates read only 250 to 300 words per minute, and remember less than 10 percent a few hours later. The solution: learn how to speed-read. With practice, you can learn to force your eyes to follow the tip of your fingers as you scan the text, thereby dramatically increasing the speed at which you read and also your level of retention. You can expect to increase your speed up to 10 TIMES with only a few hours of instruction. Some grade 12 students in Canada have been able to read **60,000 words in a minute!**—more than this whole book! There are few skills you can learn that will have as much an impact on your life as speed-reading.

Invariably, quantum leaps are not a result of any complex maneuver. They tend to be simple and energy efficient. For example, how many of us operate as if our success is certain? How many of us focus on the possibilities rather than on the problems and set-backs that confront us? None of us knows what our limitations in life really are. Most of us cling tightly to our preconceived beliefs—our life-long security blanket. Here are some ways we can use our mind to much greater effect:

*Be not
simply good;
be good for
something.*

HENRY DAVID THOREAU
AMERICAN NATURALIST,
PHILOSOPHER AND WRITER
(1817-1862)

TOOL #1

SUSPEND ALL DISBELIEF while pursuing your goal, and *act as if* it were impossible to fail. Take a quantum leap in faith—in your personal belief system that says if anyone can do it, you can! Only a quantum leap in faith can lead to a quantum leap in results.

As an exercise, take a piece of paper and write across the top a particular goal you may have. Now draw a vertical line down the middle of the page. On the right-hand side, write down all the reasons why you believe you CAN achieve your goal. On the left-hand side, write down all the reasons why you believe you CANNOT. Take your time, and exhaust all your ideas in both columns.

Now, analyze each reason on the left and see how valid it is. How valid, really, are such statements that say you don't have the time, the knowledge, the skills, the contacts, the energy . . .? If we said such things from the time we were born, where would we be today? After dealing with all the items on the left, and eliminating them, direct your focus to all the items on the right. Now ask yourself: "With only these items still having any credibility, how can I not succeed?"

Dorothea Brande was an aspiring writer back in the 1930s. But she felt she wasn't reaching anywhere near her full potential. During 20 years of work, she completed 17 short stories, 20 book reviews, half a dozen newspaper articles, and one attempt at a novel which was later abandoned. An average of only two completed pieces of work per year. But she had no idea what was holding her back, what was blocking her creative talent and energy.

As she recounts in her wonderful book *Wake Up and Live,* she witnessed what she considered was an amazing display of ability by an average person under hypnosis. Later she read that such feats were possible by hypnotized subjects because past remembrances of limitation and failure were completely erased from their memory. She reasoned that similar results could be achieved as well by average people in the wakeful state if they simply ignored their past and ACTED AS IF they could not fail.

We can act
as if there were a God; feel
as if we were free; consider Nature
as if she were full of
special designs; lay plans
as if we were to be immortal;
and we find then
that these words do make a
genuine difference in
our moral life.

WILLIAM JAMES
AMERICAN PSYCHOLOGIST
AND PHILOSOPHER
(1842-1910)

So she began to act on the assumption that she already possessed the necessary qualities and abilities she doubted she had, and aggressively forged ahead. With unabiding faith in herself, she reached a level of success and accomplishment she never dreamed was possible. In two short years after her new "discovery," she wrote three successful books, 24 articles, four short stories, outlines for three more books, and innumerable letters of consultation and professional advice that were sent to all parts of the country. Not to mention giving 72 lectures in her spare time!

TOOL #2

USE FEAR AS A POWER TOOL, as a useful device rather than as something to avoid. Fear can be controlled and directed for positive results if we learn more about its origins and features.

Human beings have a built-in, biological response to perceived danger. It's called the "fight or flight" response. Our predecessors, the cave dwellers, who could fight the hardest or run the fastest were the ones who survived. They used fear as a power tool to stay alive. And we inherited their genetic make-up.

When our body feels fear, adrenaline, glucose and other chemicals are released into the bloodstream to support the fight-flight response. Hence we get an extra burst of energy, our senses are sharpened, our minds are more alert and we can concentrate better. However, most of the fears we encounter in our daily life today are only perceived threats—they are not real threats at all. Examples: fear of heights, elevators, public speaking, snakes or air travel. As has been said, most fears are simply False Evidence Appearing Real (F.E.A.R.). The fear exists only IN OUR MIND but it often succeeds in terrorizing and immobilizing us, and all of these valuable physical and emotional benefits are wasted.

The trick then is to use fear as a power tool, to see it as a friend rather than as a foe, in helping us get what we want. In this way, we can find the extra energy and sharpened senses we need to apply to the task and challenge at hand, such as speaking in public. We simply "turn the tables" on fear and use it to our advantage.

*We are trampled
most often by forces
we ourselves
create.*

WILLIAM SHAKESPEARE
ENGLISH POET AND DRAMATIST
(1564-1616)

There is a rational explanation for the phenomenon known as "stage fright." What people are really afraid of is the humiliation and embarrassment that would follow failure. This perceived threat then automatically triggers the fight or flight response. Our muscles become taut and we tremble; our face grows pale as blood leaves the skin so we won't bleed to death if wounded; our heart starts to pound to give us more strength. At the same time, our glands shoot adrenaline into our blood stream to make us more alert, and our mouth goes dry so we won't choke on our saliva. So we see that our nervous system does everything it needs to do to help us succeed or fail, depending on how we choose to respond.

In the context of public speaking, stress provides the edge which can make the difference between an outstanding performance and a mediocre one. All veteran speakers and actors will testify that they could never perform at the level they do if stage fright was not present to lift them to a higher level of intensity. The goal then is not to focus on the stress in an attempt to make it go away. The goal is to accept and direct the stress in a positive way to improve performance.

How to Overcome F.E.A.R.

If you are prone to fears, phobias or panic attacks of one kind or another, the following may help you. A caution, however. This information should never be a substitute for professional medical advice, depending on the seriousness of the particular problem you may have.

On entering a fearful situation, we tend to see only that which we think we will see. Most fears are the result of faulty perception. The reason fearful thoughts exist at all is because our consciousness is restricted, and it sees only what we tell it to look for. Again, this is the process of selective perception at work. The remedy, rather than try to cast out something that's not really there anyway, is to expand our consciousness and begin to see some things that we have chosen to ignore.

The sorcery and charm
of imagination,
and the power it gives
to the individual to transform
his world into a new world
of order and delight, makes it one
of the most treasured
of all human capacities.

FRANK BARRON
AMERICAN PROFESSOR OF PSYCHOLOGY

Fear is not inherent in a given circumstance; it is our mental reaction to a given circumstance, to the pictures we put in our head.
If we wish to conquer fear, we must develop an ability to see safety
and control in those situations we previously found fearful and
threatening. Here are some steps to this end:

1. Relax your body (and hence your mind) by slow, controlled deep
   breathing and flexing-unflexing of the muscles. Become acutely
   aware of air s l o w l y entering your nostrils, filling your lungs,
   then s l o w l y being exhaled.
2. Scramble all the pictures in your head so that they make no sense
   whatsoever.
3. Reframe the "pictures" you have in your mind into ANYTHING
   other than the ones you had there before. One idea is to totally concentrate on what is happening in the present moment—such as
   your breathing, or what is happening around you. Another is to
   focus on only pleasant thoughts—recall the serenity of being at the
   beach; another is to concentrate intensely on . . . nothing! Try to
   eliminate all thoughts from your mind. Of course, you can't do it
   but it's fun to try.
4. Concentrate totally on these new thoughts or pictures until you become "lost" in them.
5. Repeat steps 1 to 4 above as often as necessary.

Understanding the origins of fear and how to deal with it is not a
result of any recent breakthrough in modern psychology. As Marcus
Aurelius (121-180 A.D.), the oft-quoted Stoic philosopher and
Emperor of Rome, once said, "If you are distressed by anything external, the pain is not due to the thing itself but to your own esti-
mate of it; and this you have the power to revoke at any time."

Remember you don't need a great deal of strength to let go of
something, especially something that isn't really there in the first
place. So experience the fearful thought, then just let it go. Don't

The first and best victory
is to conquer self; to be conquered
by self is of all things,
the most shameful and vile.

PLATO
GREEK PHILOSOPHER
(427-347 B.C.)

try to force it to go away, for if you keep focusing on what you don't want, you'll only get more of it. Just focus on another thought, a more pleasant one of your own choosing.

Most of us are like the proverbial housefly banging against a window. We're also locked in a glass room known as our comfort zone, and we buzz around hitting our head against the walls. We can see outside, and know what we want to do and where we want to go, but we can't break through the invisible barrier. We end up exhausted, crumpled, like the fly, just inside the point where our freedom could have begun.

When we have found a methodology to break through our fears, any fear, and find total freedom, we truly are poised for a quantum leap in performance and a new reality! Stay tuned. We've only just begun!

*All truth exists within man
and never in the world about him.
He who studies the world studies effects.
He who studies his own mind
studies the cause and source
of things as they really are.*

U. S. ANDERSEN
FROM *THREE MAGIC WORDS*

YOU HAVE TO SET YOURSELF ON F-I-R-E!

JIM ABBOTT

Jim Abbott was born in Flint, Michigan in 1967 with only a thumb for a right hand. But this didn't stop him from doing what he wanted to do—be a professional athlete. As a child, Jim spent many hours pitching imaginary baseballs in his mind. By age 11, he was pitching no-hitters for his Little League team. "I had to do it with one hand because that's all I had," he says when describing how he switches his glove back and forth so he can catch.

At Flint High School, Jim was both quarterback of the football team and captain of the baseball team. As pitcher for the University of Michigan in 1987, he won the Sullivan Award as America's best amateur athlete. In 1988, Jim pitched Team U.S.A. to the gold medal at the Seoul summer Olympics. Then, in 1989, he was one of the few pitchers to go straight from college to major league baseball when he was drafted number one by the California Angels. In 1993, he joined the legendary New York Yankees.

To what does Jim credit his success? He says, "I was lucky when I was young. My coaches, teachers, team members and my parents encouraged me. They didn't hold me back." He explains that his parents let him dream of anything. "Growing up, I always pictured myself as a baseball player, but I can't remember how many hands I had in my dreams. I never thought to myself, 'Wow, I only have one hand.'" Jim focused on his abilities, not his disabilities.

So what has happened lately to this fellow with the 94-mile-an-hour fastball? On May 29, 1993, Jim was pitching a no-hitter for the Yankees in the eighth inning when Bo Jackson of the Chicago White Sox hit a single over second base. Did this "defeat" discourage him? Well, only weeks later, on September 4, Jim pitched a 4 to 0 no-hitter against the Cleveland Indians. How is that for an encore! No one can predict what level of success Jim will reach.

You make a difference by giving something of yourself for the betterment of others. Jim Abbott has made a difference. He dared to dream big dreams, and in the process, he set himself on fire!

I tried to
change my life
once. It didn't work, so
I gave up.

ARCHIE BUNKER
FROM THE AMERICAN SITCOM
"ALL IN THE FAMILY"

CHAPTER 7

The Power of Belief

Man is what he believes.
—Anton Chekhov

Belief: The Mother of Creation

All reality, all things, are rooted in faith, in our beliefs that we accept as firm convictions, often based on little understanding and no evidence. We assume that the planet will always turn, the sun will always shine, and flowers will always bloom. We even believe we are alive! But how can we be certain of this if we have never been alive—or dead—before? We assume we're alive because other people say we are, but they are as ignorant about the matter as we are.

Faith is blind. Sustained by the substance of things hoped for and the evidence of things not seen, great men and women have set out on perilous and uncertain journeys to follow their dreams. Inventors invent; explorers explore; builders build; writers write; singers sing; dancers dance. All are achievers who believe, who persist in their quest on faith and faith alone.

As we have seen, the primary role of the Subconscious Mind is to take ideas, thoughts and concepts in the mental world and go about transforming them into their physical counterparts. It is the master creator, always manifesting. But it only acts on certainties or absolutes passed on to it from the Conscious Mind. It exercises no judgment, no assessment as to the origin, appropriateness or validity of the information. It acts equally upon all certainties, all accepted truths, all firm convictions presented to it—what we consciously accept as "IS."

Not all of our thoughts have the power to create our reality. If they did, we would be creating thousands of conflicting and often irrelevant "facts" every day of our life. Clearly there is great selectivity being exercised on a regular basis concerning which thoughts in the

Whatever you vividly imagine,
ardently desire,
and enthusiastically act upon,
must inevitably come to pass.

NAPOLEON HILL
AUTHOR OF *THINK AND GROW RICH*
(1883-1970)

Conscious Mind are to be accepted and passed on to the Subconscious. Equally apparent is that all such selection is carried out, not by the Subconscious, but by the Conscious Mind.

This is evident by observing a person under hypnosis. The Subconscious Mind of such a person readily accepts any premise presented to it by an outside party. If told that the left arm has no feeling, then the left arm has no feeling. If told the temperature in the room is 120 degrees, then the hypnotized person responds immediately and begins to perspire. Hypnosis "deactivates" or disconnects the Conscious Mind from the normal thinking process, and hence all evaluation and selection of thoughts is negated. All suggestions from the outside therefore proceed directly to the Subconscious Mind where they are accepted without question.

The Impetus of Conviction

The only reason all our thoughts are not turned into physical reality is because they are not CONVICTIONS of the Conscious Mind. For only if they are convictions are they sent to the Subconscious to be acted upon. Thus all our convictions, or core beliefs, are turned into form and we can neither start nor stop this process. It happens automatically. The Subconscious is always creating. This is its nature. It is always in the "transformation" mode. The only thing we can control are the thoughts we pass on, the things we decide to believe in or not believe in at the conscious level.

We now can see why belief is such a powerful factor in our life. **Belief gives the impetus of conviction to a thought,** and thereby impresses the thought upon the Subconscious Mind as a premise or outcome that MUST BE BROUGHT INTO REALITY. Hence anything we are thoroughly convinced of must eventually become real in our life.

Of course, if we had been built as mechanical robots under the control of some omnipotent being who made all the choices, faith would have no role to play. Our master would simply direct to our Subconscious all the appropriate commands that represented his will, and their effects would quickly follow. But we were not created this way. Our existence was put in our hands. We have been given the

(continued on page 205)

It's much more difficult to defeat an opponent who has made up his mind that he's going to win, no matter what.

"THE SPORTS CLINIC"

DEVELOPING MENTAL FITNESS

If you are an athlete or an aspiring athlete, amateur or professional, consider the importance of belief—of total CONVICTION!—as it affects your performance.

Whatever the sport—swimming, tennis, baseball, hockey, figure skating, basketball, football or volleyball, you practice elements of the sport until you master the fundamentals. You do this both physically and mentally—by actually playing the game in real-life situations and visualizing playing the game in your mind. The object in both cases is to train your mind and nervous system to do what you want your physical body to do.

With enough practice, you'll master the skills to a level commensurate with your natural abilities. This doesn't mean you'll perform perfectly every time. It only means that you have demonstrated the ability to do what you are physically able to do on a fairly consistent basis when you are in your most empowered state.

Belief largely determines whether you are in your most empowered state or not. You know through experience that your performance can be inconsistent, but you don't always know why. Deep down in your Subconscious Mind, you know things can go either way in an actual game scenario. On some occasions, you do things right. On others, you don't. So ask yourself: where does your mind go, on what does it focus in key situations? If you allow your mind to entertain the possibility of failure . . . then, of course, you open up the possibility of failure occurring.

"THE SPORTS CLINIC"
(continued)

Imagine you are a pitcher on a baseball team about to start a critical game. You wonder if you can win the game. But consider this—who do you really have to convince that you're going to be successful? Yes, YOU!

There is a sort of mental "magic" that occurs when the mind entertains the possibility of only ONE OUTCOME. Your thought processes and whole nervous system direct all their efforts to bring about this one outcome.

Can you "psyche" yourself up to perform at a higher level—at will? Of course you can. You repeat the appropriate words to yourself—"I can! I can! I can!" along with matching vivid visualizations of the performance you desire. You then adopt the appropriate physiology—muscle tone, facial features, body posture and breathing pattern—commensurate with this peak state. In brief, to be empowered, you must *say* it, *"see"* it, and *feel* it throughout your whole body—the "it" being the precise performance you want. AND DO NOT ALLOW YOUR MIND TO ENTERTAIN ANY THOUGHTS TO THE CONTRARY! Send them to oblivion! Winners think only about winning.

Beliefs affect our mind and body "chemistry" in many ways. The result is a calm assuredness, an inner certainty of the outcome. The desired mental and physical effects of being in your most resourceful state include: greater intensity, more focus, and better concentration; more strength and energy; and unlimited persistence and determination to succeed.

Athletes have to have as many things going for them as they can in an effort to get more consistent and more successful results. If sports contests are 90 percent mental and 10 percent physical—which I believe to be true, then mastering the mental aspect is absolutely essential. It's a matter of sitting down before the event and sorting out all your thoughts, then agreeing to focus on only those thoughts that are consistent with the one outcome you have decided you want.

If you want a quality,
act as if
you already had it.
Try the
"as if" technique.

WILLIAM JAMES
AMERICAN PSYCHOLOGIST
AND PHILOSOPHER
(1842-1910)

responsibility to decide, to choose our own convictions, to determine what reality we want to create.

All things, both good and evil, have their beginnings in faith. If the Subconscious receives our conviction that we'll earn a specific sum of money by a certain date by performing a certain task, it immediately goes to work to help bring this about. It sends a multitude of hidden prompters to show us the way. If our conviction is that we are competent, capable and deserving, so shall we also be moved in this direction.

Exercise

Having "faith" is not a simple business. It's easy to believe something if you already believe it. And it's not easy to believe something if you already don't believe it. But assuming you really want to believe this "something," just how do you summon up the necessary "faith" to do it? Answer: You **ACT AS IF** you have the faith—you pretend—and move forward. What you certainly don't want to do is sit and dwell on the matter, and let the hidden prompters in your mind wage a war that usually results, at best, in a draw. As Sally Kempton has remarked, "It's hard to fight an enemy who has outposts in your head."

This brings us to something I call the **Fail-Proof Formula for Success.** The mind has to know and understand that there is a rational way to proceed in a given direction if considerable risk is involved. So here is the logic. Instance #1. Let's assume you believe that you can do something you want to do. So you begin to take the necessary steps—you initiate some ACTION—in the required direction that starts to get some results that in turn reinforces your original belief. You are on your way.

Now consider Instance #2. In this case, let's assume you are NOT convinced that you can do something you want to do. So you decide to just ASSUME you can—you pretend—and begin to take the necessary steps in the required direction AS IF YOU DID BELIEVE YOU COULD—the same steps as above—and guess what? You start to get the same results as in Instance #1, which in turn begins to build true belief in your ability. Again, you are on your way!

*The thing always happens
that you really believe in;
and the belief in a thing
makes it happen.*

FRANK LLOYD WRIGHT
AMERICAN ARCHITECT
(1869-1959)

Either approach, then, gets you where you want to go. But it's critical to understand that in either instance, whether you believe you CAN do something or believe you CANNOT but choose to proceed as if you did, you can't build belief or change your beliefs about anything unless you follow through with ACTION!

This one simple concept—the Fail-Proof Formula for Success—is a success system that can never fail. By itself, it has the potential to turn your life around. Why? Because all success must include these three essential elements: you must

1. know what you want;
2. believe you can get it—have faith; and
3. take action in the direction you want to go.

Many people know what they want. But since they don't believe they can get it, they don't take any action to that end. Hence everything grinds to a complete halt. This concept—acting as if you believed—gets you past the doubt barrier and into the action mode. BECAUSE NOW YOU BELIEVE THAT IF YOU PRETEND YOU BELIEVE AND TAKE THE NECESSARY ACTION, YOU WILL GET THE SAME RESULTS AS THOUGH YOU DID BELIEVE! Now you have the required faith that you will achieve the desired outcome.

Assume that I suggest you affirm the following simple statement to yourself as a way to positively impact your Subconscious Mind: "I am healthy; I am wealthy; I am wise." If you repeat this phrase or affirmation over and over again to yourself several times a day every day for at least 30 days, you are certain to become healthier, wealthier and wiser.

What, you don't believe me? Most people don't. That's why only a few will actually take this advice and do it. People who don't believe it, won't do it. Then, of course, it certainly won't work. As Benedict Spinoza has noted, "So long as a person imagines that he cannot do this or that, so long as he determines not to do it; and consequently so long is it impossible to him that he should do it."

Our doubts are traitors,
and make us lose the good
we oft might win by
fearing to attempt.

WILLIAM SHAKESPEARE
ENGLISH POET AND DRAMATIST
(1564-1616)

But even if some people are willing to do it, to try it as a test, they remain sceptical and their attempt is only half-hearted. It lacks CONVICTION! Most of their faith is directed at proving their doubts are justified. So if you initially have doubts but still want to believe in my advice, then "have faith" and do it!

People who are totally convinced of a negative outcome have total faith that it will happen. Lack of faith is not their downfall. It is having complete faith in the very thing they don't want! Similarly, those who only WISH or HOPE for a positive outcome are doomed to fail. It's because, again, their faith is really in the opposite direction, but often they're not aware of it or don't want to admit it. It's only the thought that is propelled forward by total conviction that eventually appears on the stage of reality. This is because the Subconscious creates in our experience only what we believe. We need only look at the circumstances we find ourselves in—our health, our family, our profession, our activities, our possessions, our friends—to see what kind of firm beliefs we now have.

So our beliefs are very important THINGS. They represent conscious decisions we have made in the past about ourselves and our world, and what we expect or do not expect to accomplish. As long as we don't challenge these beliefs, their effects will continue to be manifested in our life. They will continually control our thinking, direct our behavior, and determine our relative level of performance. How we perform in any given area of our life is only partly a function of our potential in that area. In fact, it's largely a function of our deep-seated beliefs.

Beliefs in turn create what we call our mental attitude. We often use the terms positive or negative—and on occasion lousy!—to describe other people's behavior or demeanor—their attitude. So exactly what is attitude, anyway, and what is the precise role that beliefs play? Well, **our mental attitude** is defined as our **habitual** manner of acting, feeling and **thinking** that shows our disposition, opinions and **beliefs** about life. The three key words are "habitual," "thinking" and "beliefs." Knowing now that the attitude we have is a direct result of the beliefs we hold, let's continue our investigation of beliefs in more detail.

*I have found
that if I have faith in myself
and in the idea I am
tinkering with, I usually
win out.*

CHARLES F. KETTERING
AMERICAN INVENTOR
(1876-1958)

Core Beliefs

Of all our beliefs, the most important are our core beliefs, for they are absolutely critical to our future. We possess thousands upon thousands of beliefs about every aspect of our life. We have an opinion or belief about golf, the environment, designer clothes, government officials, dolphins, Caribbean cruises, Coca Cola, ice cream, leather furniture, UFOs, artificial flowers, classical music, polo ponies, jumbo jets and fly fishing. But none of these particular beliefs is likely to have a major impact on our life. The same cannot be said about our core beliefs. For core beliefs are basic to our very being, and are primary determinants concerning the direction our life takes.

I'm sure you have heard the expression, "We're engineered for success but often programmed for failure." And it's absolutely true.

When we were born, we didn't know anything about anything, and hence didn't have a bunch of beliefs about anything either. Our mind was simply a blank slate. Then we experienced something of life, and learned things about ourselves and our world. And if we validated this same information often enough in our later experiences, we accepted it as "true" and it became part of our reality profile.

Let's take a look at how we all got here. For the first nine months of our life, we got to spend time in this wonderful place called—the womb. Now it wasn't a hotel room but it was better than a hotel room in many ways because: the room temperature was just right; room service was 24 hours a day; tipping was not allowed; and we had the very latest in bedding—a wall-to-wall water-bed! In fact, we never had to get out of bed. Things couldn't have been more perfect until, for some reason, we got evicted. Now we don't know why—whether we got too rowdy or behind on the rent—but out we went. The first thing that happened was someone wearing a mask grabbed us by our two feet, turned us upside down, and gave us a smart whack on the behind. Then this person cut our umbilical cord and tied it in a tight little knot. Hard to believe, perhaps, but this was our welcome to the real world! And for many of us, it never got any better.

Nothing has
any power over me
other than
that which I give it
through my
conscious thoughts.

ANTHONY ROBBINS
FROM *UNLIMITED POWER*

The problem is that as we grew up, we allowed ourselves to be conditioned to a remarkable extent by our environment to believe many things about ourselves and our world that are simply not true. This shouldn't be a big surprise. We adopted the majority of our beliefs at a very young age, at a time when we weren't that well informed about anything. We simply weren't in the best position to make important decisions that would stay with us for the rest of our life.

Think of it. For the first three or four years of our life, we never exceeded three feet in height. Hence all we saw at eye level were the fannies of all the adults around us. Clearly it's impossible to develop a positive perspective about life from this particular vantage point!

So look at the following set of core beliefs as one that is available to you. Of course, you must have one set of core beliefs or another, hence it's only prudent that you adopt one that empowers and energizes you rather than limits and deflates you.

These core beliefs are unique to all peak performing men and women. We know that if we want to get the results that winners get, **we must first think like a winner thinks!** Consider each one of these beliefs carefully, and imagine what your world would begin to look like if you held the same beliefs and made them a part of your life today.

*1. Winners are **made**, not born.*

At birth, we were given a magnificent computer for our personal use—but no software of any kind to run it! We lacked the particular beliefs, knowledge and insight we need to succeed in life. But this we can acquire at any time, if we choose to do so. Success is a journey, a trip that only we can take, one step at a time.

IMPLICATION: Life is a "do-it-yourself" project. Adopt the philosophy, "If it is to be, it's up to me." Surely you didn't think someone else was going to do it for you!

*The belief that comes true for me . . .
is that which allows me the best use
of my strength, the best means
of putting my virtues into action.*

ANDRE GIDE
FRENCH AUTHOR AND CRITIC
(1869-1951)

*2. The dominant force in our existence is the **thinking** we engage in on a daily basis.*

Life is an inner game. All causation is mental. We succeed from the inside out. We become what we think about all the time.

IMPLICATION: Be very careful about the thinking you engage in. For as you think, so you become.

*3. We are empowered to create our own **reality**—of who we are and what kind of world we live in.*

Our five senses perceive the world in the best way they can. But it's our brain that interprets this input and gives it its meaning. Would you rather have something or someone else decide its meaning for you?

IMPLICATION: Be aware of the reality you create. Does it make sense to have drawn the conclusions you have about yourself based solely on the current evidence? Absence of evidence of something is not necessarily evidence of its absence.

*4. There is some **benefit** to be had from every adversity.*

Adversity is a great teacher. It tells us that something doesn't work. But in the process of finding this out, we learn something. And this is the great benefit—so long as we change our approach, and "keep on keeping on" until we get the results we want.

IMPLICATION: Focus on the benefit, not on the failure.

*5. The personal belief system we now have is **total choice.***

We have a belief about everything. But no belief is an absolute, either about us or our world. A belief doesn't necessarily reflect knowledge. More often than not, it reflects a lack of knowledge. For example, everyone once thought the world was flat—until Columbus came along and proved otherwise. We need only believe what we want to believe about ourselves and the world we live in, and then go out and prove that we're right!

In the province of the mind,
what one believes to be true
either is true or
becomes true.

JOHN LILLY
AMERICAN AUTHOR, EDUCATOR
AND PHYSICIAN
(1915-1962)

IMPLICATION: Select core beliefs that empower you and help you move ahead, rather than ones that limit you and hold you back.

*6. We are **never defeated** until we accept defeat as a reality, and decide to stop trying.*

Defeat and failure are relative. They are only part of life's great journey. They have no meaning or relevancy—unless we decide to give them meaning and relevancy.

IMPLICATION: Never give up and you will succeed. Remember, winners never quit and quitters never win.

*7. We already possess the ability to **excel** in at least one key area of our life.*

A study at Harvard University found that everyone is a potential genius—at something. But it remains for us to apply ourselves and find out what this area is. Genius is only the ability to think in unconventional ways. When everyone thinks alike, no one is thinking at all. Choose this unconventional thought: believe that you can become outstanding in your chosen field of endeavour. If you do, you'll be in the top one percent of the population.

IMPLICATION: Find out what you're good at. Often it's something you love to do, that gives you the greatest satisfaction and sense of importance. Otherwise, just DECIDE what it is you want to excel at. Then go out and do it!

*8. The only real limitations on what we can accomplish in our life are those **we impose on ourself**.*

We have to decide if any limitations on our potential exist. No one can label us a failure without our consent. Remember: the world forms its opinion of us primarily from the opinion we already have of ourself.

IMPLICATION: The only way to discover your limitations is to go beyond them. Assume no limitations. Who are you to know, anyway? So get on with the task.

*Creativity can solve
almost any problem.
The creative act,
the defeat of habit
by originality,
overcomes everything.*

GEORGE LOIS
AMERICAN AUTHOR
AND ADVERTISING EXECUTIVE

*9. There can be no great success without **great commitment.***

If we are going to become outstanding at anything, we have to—surprise!—work at it. We have to pay the price. We get nothing by doing nothing. We get out of anything only in proportion to what we put in. And there is no limit to what we can put in!

IMPLICATION: Commitment is a function of your belief and desire. Work on these two, and commitment automatically will follow.

*10. We need the support and cooperation of **other people** to achieve any worthwhile goal.*

No one functions in a vacuum. We are all part of families, work in organizations, and live in communities. Many people with different specialties must come together in the pursuit of common objectives. It necessarily follows that the better the support and the better the cooperation, the better the results will be.

IMPLICATION: Find out how to establish and maintain effective and productive interpersonal relationships.

I suggest these core beliefs are a more accurate and realistic representation of your True Self than your current beliefs that represent your Artificial Self. And if you program such beliefs deep into your subconscious reality—your inner consciousness, they will eventually be manifested in your life. Simply put, consciously believing and "seeing" is the key to achieving.

Habitual Thinking

You may wonder why more people don't already have winning core beliefs. Again, we come back to the real world we live in. It has been estimated that we have at least 50,000 thoughts a day, at most 5,000 thoughts an hour. I ask you: how many of the thoughts that you have in a given day are positive? If it's 50 percent, this only balances off the 50 percent that are negative, and you go nowhere. You must get well above 50 percent, I believe close to 80 or 90 percent, before you can hope to make any real progress. And this can be done only by controlling your thoughts one at a time.

Believe nothing,
no matter where you read it,
or who said it
—even if I have said it—
unless it agrees
with your own reason and
your own common sense.

BUDDHA
RELIGIOUS TEACHER
(563-483 B.C.)

Thought control simply means thinking the one thing you want and not thinking the opposite. This is not an easy feat for most of us because we have practiced negative thinking for all of our life. We just assumed we never had a choice. In fact, most people would consider any attempt to banish negative thoughts from their mind as sheer folly. They think that negative thoughts are just too powerful. But are they?

Negative thinking is just another habit. A habit is simply the result of thinking in a habitual way. So if we think in a different way, we can break the habit, any habit, like smoking. Is breaking a habit easy? Not for a lot of people. At the same time, it's easy for many others. Of course to succeed requires commitment to do the thing, to see it through, believing we will be better off not having the habit than to continue having it. This is where many people fail. They don't accept the notion that to rid themselves of negative thinking is worth the effort required to do it. Often it takes what in psychology is called a significant emotional event (or S.E.E.) to shake their complacency. For example, a smoker who has just had a heart attack or a black spot found on her lung is, not surprisingly, a lot more open to rethinking her stance on smoking! So think about it—just how miserable do you want to get before you're willing to take some steps to turn your life around?

Where Do Thoughts Come From?

Most people are under the illusion that THEY THINK! In other words, they believe that they literally MAKE thoughts. Nothing could be further from the truth. No one has ever been able to say how a thought is made, what it looks like, or where it comes from or travels to after use. In fact, all thoughts that have ever been or ever will be have already been created. They exist as spirit. They represent universal intelligence that each of us can access through our Subconscious Mind.

By carefully analyzing the process of thinking, we find we are not the creator but rather the observer of thoughts as they flip into and

Sooner or later every one
of us breathes an atom that
has been breathed before
by anyone you can think of—
Michelangelo or George Washington
or Moses.

JACOB BRONOWSKI
ENGLISH SCIENTIST AND PHILOSOPHER
(1908-1974)

out of our consciousness. Our minds are like large receiving stations that attract thoughts that parade across our consciousness in a never-ending stream, much like the dots and dashes of Morse code. And we, from the vantage point of our Conscious Mind, are like innocent observers of the whole process, watching all the activity quite innocently from a distance. As we become aware of some thoughts, we can slow them down and dwell on them. Others we can simply acknowledge with a curt salute and send on their way. But we are not the ones who have set the stream of thoughts in motion. And we cannot turn the stream off no matter how hard we try.

A good analogy is perhaps a garden hose that is turned on full. By controlling the nozzle, we can slow the flow down or speed it up, or point the flow in a particular direction, say up—positive, or down—negative. For example, I didn't sit down and "create" any of the thoughts that make up this book myself. I simply turned on the valve, controlled the flow, and pointed my thoughts in a particular direction. If I found a thought I liked, I selected and recorded it. All the others I discarded as not being relevant, and just let them continue on their journey. After all, they may well be of use to someone else! (Gee, where did I get this idea about the garden hose, anyway?)

Of course, following this process, I didn't "think up" a thing. The result, when assembled and written down, is simply evidence of the thousands of choices I made from all the thoughts that passed my way. It tells you a great deal about the thoughts I selected, but of course it tells you very little about the many I rejected.

A Traffic Cop

We are the only one in constant communication with ourselves. We act like a traffic cop. We are the only one who can police the thoughts and control the images we put in our head. If we allow in images to impact and direct us at random, then we're not in control. But if our focus is primarily on only those thoughts and images that are in accordance with our deep-seated desires and aspirations, then we are creating the sort of life we want. We may not be able to stop

*The last of
the human freedoms is
to choose one's attitude
in any given
set of circumstances—
to choose one's own way.*

VIKTOR E. FRANKL
AUTHOR OF *MAN'S SEARCH
FOR MEANING*

the earth from rotating or alter the position of a star, but we can choose our current dominant thoughts, what we think about, in spite of what the world is telling us.

The positive or negative aspect of any thought, of course, depends on how we interpret or "frame" it. Let's assume you are haunted by things you did or didn't do in the past. We all have some regrets we would rather not dwell on. But if you put the following "frame" around such thoughts—everything happens for a reason and a purpose, and it serves us—then the sting of its recollection is likely to be less severe. Or you could say "Well, yes, I didn't do everything that I should have. You win some and you lose some. But I'm still batting over 500, and there's no one in professional baseball that can say that!"

Or assume that you stuttered as a child, and have lacked self-confidence ever since as a result. Research will tell you that Sir Isaac Newton, Sir Winston Churchill, King George VI, Somerset Maugham, Charles Darwin and Aristotle also stuttered in their youth. So you could mentally degrade yourself because of this affliction, or alternatively upgrade yourself by associating yourself in your mind with others who have also been stutterers. Is this such a bad group of people to associate yourself with? If this is a genetic defect, maybe it's one you want! The same can be said about almost any so-called "limiting" characteristic, be it physical or mental.

We are all impacted by events in our life, some of which we can control and others that we cannot. The critical question is not whether we can control a particular event. It's our reaction to it— the frame we put around it—that's most important. **It is our response to an event that determines its impact on us.** Only we can push the buttons on our computer keyboard that then determine the meaning of everything in our life.

For example, for many people in pursuit of a goal, the concept of failure does not compute. It has no meaning. They simply see it as a learning experience, a sign of progress, as a pebble along the road. In a very real sense, because we can exercise total control over our thoughts, we have total control over our life—if we learn how to respond creatively and positively to events, especially those that are unexpected or at first glance seem undesirable.

*Faced with the choice
between changing one's mind
and proving there is
no need to do so,
almost everyone gets busy
on the proof.*

JOHN KENNETH GALBRAITH
CANADIAN-BORN POLITICAL
COMMENTATOR

Remember: only thoughts can stop us from moving in new directions—our thoughts! It's positive thoughts that lead to positive beliefs that lead to positive results. We don't want to blow with the wind and be manipulated by any old thought that just comes our way. We don't want to be left to the whims of fate. We want control—and control comes from exercising our "response-ability."

Life is a harsh teacher if we let it consume us at will. We have to stand up and be counted if we want to effect the changes that are important to us. In this journey, we have two choices. We can go merrily along, and learn from our own mistakes. This path is time-consuming and holds many pitfalls. Or we can learn from the mistakes of others, those who have gone before us and found what works and what doesn't.

We need to ask ourself this question: "Is there anything I can't learn more about in order to do it better?" Of course not. There are secrets to success . . . but none that cannot be discovered through an aggressive search. More information is available today on how to be successful in life than ever before. Books, audio and video cassettes, lectures and public seminars are available to all, usually at modest prices and sometimes even free at your local public library.

We need only access this information to move ahead quickly in our life. Don't wait for this information to seek you out. It cannot. You must be the aggressor in this mighty quest. Discovering the beliefs of the world's super achievers—those who take purposeful action, and adopting them as your own is a good place to start. As some wise person once remarked, "The problem with learning only from the school of hard knocks is that by the time you're ready to graduate, you're also about ready to die!" The best investment you can make is in yourself, in discovering your unique talents and abilities, and developing them to make your life more vibrant, more exciting and more meaningful.

*You have
the phenomenal power
to live your dreams,
if you will only
control
your thoughts.*

WALLY "FAMOUS" AMOS
FOUNDER OF FAMOUS AMOS
CHOCOLATE CHIP COOKIES

YOU HAVE TO SET YOURSELF ON F-I-R-E!

HELEN KELLER

Helen Keller was born on June 27, 1880, in a small town in Alabama. In February, 1882, when she was one and a half years old, Helen was struck with an unknown illness, experiencing a very high fever and severe pain. When she finally recovered, she was both deaf and blind.

When Helen was seven, her father arranged for a tutor, Anne Sullivan, to move in with the family. Anne eventually taught Helen how to communicate using finger movements, how to read by Braille, and eventually how to speak. Helen was among the very first with her particular impediments to master these skills. Anne Sullivan was her constant companion for the next fifty years.

What did Helen do with her life, despite her seemingly insurmountable handicaps? She graduated from Radcliffe College in 1904 with honors, alongside some of the most brilliant young women of her time. She became an accomplished public speaker and social critic, passionately dedicating her life to helping disadvantaged groups such as the poor, the homeless and the less fortunate. She wrote five books, and claimed as close friends many notables of the day including Alexander Graham Bell, Mark Twain, Albert Einstein and Charlie Chaplain. She met with the kings and queens of Europe and every U.S. president of her life-time. At age 75, she was the first woman to receive an honorary degree from Harvard University. Three films were made about her life.

Helen died on June 1, 1968. She remains to this day a shining example to millions of people that so much can be accomplished in life even if you start with so little. You need only look beyond obvious limitations to what is possible, to what is important, to what is needed.

You make a difference by giving something of yourself for the betterment of others. Helen Keller has made a difference. She dared to dream big dreams, and in the process, she set herself on fire!

Men and women
who have achieved greatness
all have one thing in common . . .
they believed they could make it.
This belief, and the tenacious
determination it inspires,
is a necessary element for success.

JIM ROHN
AUTHOR AND MOTIVATIONAL SPEAKER

CHAPTER 8

How to Change Core Beliefs

*What we have to do is to be forever curiously testing
new opinions and courting new impressions.*
— Walter Pater

Steps to Creating New Beliefs

We know that each of our core beliefs is a choice, and that new core beliefs offer a unique opportunity for a quantum leap in our performance. So what are some of the ways we can change our core beliefs, and move ahead with our life? Here are eight proven ways that can be used individually or collectively to change our basic beliefs about ourselves and our world:

1. Practice original thinking, which is the critical reassessment of long-standing beliefs. Take a certain belief you now have about yourself, and ask

> Why do I have it?
> How valid is it?
> Who says so?
> What are their credentials for knowing so
> much about me?
> Is this belief still relevant today?

If you now firmly believe—"I could never hope to be, to do or to have . . . whatever," then seriously question it! It's called RE-THINK!

> We are who we are because of what we believe.
> We can change who we are by changing what we believe.

2. Change the words you say to yourself, your self-talk. Stop saying negative things to yourself. It only tears you down. Restate the same comment in exactly the opposite way, and notice the positive effect it has on you. "I can't speak in public because . . . " becomes "I can

---

231

The greatest obstacle
to discovery
is not ignorance—
it is the illusion
of knowledge.

DANIEL J. BOORSTIN
AMERICAN AUTHOR

speak in public because . . . " Be your own best cheerleader: "I'm the best! I'm the best! I'm the best! I can do it! I can do it! I can do it!" BECAUSE YOU CAN!

3. Change the pictures you have in your head about yourself—by using your imagination. Can you see yourself succeeding at something you already know you are very good at? Now use the same process to see yourself succeeding at something you WANT to be very good at. The process is this simple. Here is a startling fact: a picture imagined vividly, earnestly and in every detail in your mind can have 10 to 60 times more impact on the brain than a real-life experience! You can literally "imagine" your way to success! And we know nothing succeeds like success.

4. Change your physiology to get the behavior you want. Your physiology includes your tone of voice, your facial features, your body posture, your muscle tone, and your breathing pattern. Your muscles have memory. You have developed a physiology for positive emotions such as happiness, excitement, peace of mind, and self-confidence. As well, you have developed a particular physiology for negative emotions such as sadness, boredom, depression, anxiety, and self-doubt. You need only choose the particular feeling you want, then adjust your physiology accordingly.

5. Change the information you expose yourself to by reading motivational books, going to motivational seminars, and listening to motivational tapes. Use the power of the suggestive elements in your life to excite you rather than depress you. Be a lifelong student of the subject of success.

First we need to learn to read; then we need to read to learn. Books contain the wisdom of the ages. Use them to get the knowledge you need to become excellent at what you do. Mark Twain once said, "The person who does not read good books has no advantage over the person who cannot read." And it was Walter Staples who said, "Not to know is forgivable. Not to want to know is not."

Did you know that the average adult reads less than one book a year, that 58 percent of all adults never read another non-fiction book after high school? A recent study revealed that if you read for

*A single conversation
with a wise person
is worth a month's study
of books.*

OLD CHINESE PROVERB

only 60 minutes a day—about one book a week or 52 books a year—that after three years, you would be an authority in your field; after five years, certainly an expert; and after seven years, you would be at the very top of your profession. After 10 years, you would have read 520 books and acquired the knowledge of 520 other recognized authorities on the subject. Can you imagine what kind of advantage this would give you over your peers?

In fact, it has been said that if you read three to five books that represent the very best in their field, you would acquire 80 to 90 percent of the critical knowledge on that subject. Obvious subjects to study for most people would include health and fitness, parenting, financial planning, business books, and books that deal with personal development—popular psychology, philosophy, and biographies or autobiographies. It is the books in this last category, personal development, that will determine your progress in all the other areas. If you don't feel good about yourself, are you going to exercise and watch your diet; be a good parent; have your finances in order; or be at the very top of your profession? The answer is clear—NO!

Here is a statement that I believe is accurate: "You are the best teacher you'll ever have. If the student is ready, he'll teach himself. If he is not ready, he cannot be taught." Clearly this message applies to all learning, including personal development.

6. Associate with other successful people. Everyone you meet knows something you don't. So find out what successful people know that can be of benefit to you. How do you find out what they know? You must: 1. Ask. 2. Ask intelligently. 3. Ask the right people. 4. Ask as many people as you can. 5. Always have an open mind—be teachable. Other people, books, tapes, seminars—immerse yourself in a positive environment.

7. Take action in the area you want to be proficient in. Test what your belief system is telling you. Then assess your results, change your approach, and keep on taking action until you get the precise results you want. If you follow these simple steps, it's clear that there is no such thing as failure—there are only results. If you don't like the results you're now getting, change your approach. There is no way you can fail completely if you follow this advice.

If you would be a real seeker after truth, it is necessary at least once in your life to doubt as far as possible all things.

RENE DESCARTES
FRENCH PHILOSOPHER
AND MATHEMATICIAN
(1596-1650)

8. Act the part. If you want to be confident, act confident. If you want to be energetic, act energetic. If you want to be excited, act excited. Purposeful action triggers positive emotions that trigger positive pictures in your mind. So—ACT, ACT, ACT.

Exercises

ORIGINAL THINKING

1. In point 1 above, we suggested using original thinking to change our core beliefs. Take a long-standing belief you now have about yourself, one that seems to be holding you back, and seriously question it. First state it clearly by writing it down. Then ask yourself, "Where did I get it, how valid is it, have I ever tested it, and is it still valid today in light of new information I have?" If it doesn't pass this test, throw it away!

POSITIVE SELF-TALK

2. In point 2, we discussed the negative effect our self-talk can have on our feelings and behavior. The best way to combat this is to repeat constantly only positive affirmations to yourself, ones that apply directly to whatever challenge or opportunity is currently of importance to you. An affirmation simply frames a desired outcome in a positive way. It is a statement in the first person singular, "I"; in the present tense; and positive. You would not say, for example, "I no longer smoke." You would say, "I am a non-smoker. I am a non-smoker."

What are some affirmations you could formulate right now that would help you be more successful in various aspects of your life? Consider your level of self-confidence, financial goals, time management, memory improvement, diet and exercise, and personal relationships. If you wrote these affirmations down, where could you post them to make you more visually aware of them throughout the day? Well—on your bathroom mirror; the refrigerator door; the dash of your car; or the cover of your day-timer . . . anywhere you look a lot, like the middle of your TV screen!

So much is
a man worth
as he
esteems himself.

FRANÇOIS RABELAIS
FRENCH SATIRIST AND HUMORIST
(1494-1553)

Here are some suggested affirmations to practice daily:

• Today, I have a positive mental attitude. I have eliminated criticism and impatience from my life, and replaced them with praise and tolerance.

• Today, I totally believe in myself. I believe I am worthy and capable of high achievement.

• Today, I have a big, challenging goal that I'm working toward. It's adding meaning and momentum to my life.

• Today, I accept full responsibility for all my actions. Whatever results I achieve, I know they are the result of the thinking I engage in.

• Today, I manage my time effectively. I know every minute is precious and irreplaceable, and must be used to best advantage.

• Today, I'm pursuing a personal development program. I dedicate at least one hour each day toward improving myself.

• Today, I value myself physically, mentally and spiritually. I'm taking very good care of myself.

• Today, I am creative in the way I set and reach my goals. Possibilities abound in all my thoughts and actions.

• Today, I have a service-minded approach toward my employment and fellow human beings. I always do more than what is expected of me, knowing I will receive more of what I want in return.

• Today, I am excellent at what I do. I believe it is through excellence that I will find my True Self.

• Today, I am effective in all my interpersonal relationships. I believe people take priority over problems, and that they deserve my total respect and attention.

*Imagination
is more important
than knowledge.*

ALBERT EINSTEIN
GERMAN-BORN PHYSICIST
(1879-1955)

CREATIVE VISUALIZATION

3. In point 3, we noted that our imagination is our most powerful tool for creating a new reality. Imagination can condition our consciousness any way we choose, and of course either positively or negatively. Used properly, it can make us master of all events and all the circumstances in our life. We need no longer respond only to happenings all around us. Instead, we can cast up mental pictures in our mind that are full of sound and fury, literally pulsating with life, that depict our innermost desires. By creating these visualizations, these animations as positive and life-like, we can override all of our self-doubts and fears. We can move our consciousness in the direction of our creative visions, rather than in the direction of our sensory perceptions. We can use our inner power of vision to transcend the limiting stimuli of the outer world. We can create a reality of our own choosing.

Consider the following visualization to demonstrate how creative you can be, as well as the emotional effects that even an outlandish adventure can have. (Note: Do not practice this or any other visualization while driving an automobile.)

Close your eyes. I want you to imagine that you're standing all alone on the roof of a skyscraper in Manhattan at one o'clock in the morning. You are **110 stories** above street level. The view is incredible—you can see the lights of New York City in all directions, from Brooklyn to the Bronx. There are red lights, yellow lights, green lights and flashing neon signs so large that they are visible from 20 miles away. Now carefully walk over to the edge of the roof and look down. Can you see the headlights of all the cars, buses and taxis streaking up and down the street? You are 1,500 feet up in the air. Now there's a ledge around the roof to prevent people from inadvertently walking right off. It's about two feet high and one foot wide. I want you to put your right foot up on this ledge, very carefully, then slowly lean over and look down once again. Boy, that's a long, long way down, baby! Can you feel a slight shiver go through your body?

*The source and center
of all man's creative power is
his power of making images,
or the power of imagination.*

ROBERT COLLIER
AUTHOR OF *THE SECRET OF THE AGES*
(1885-1950)

Now I want you to take your left foot, and lift it up beside your right so that you are standing all alone on this narrow ledge. Wheee! You feel a gentle summer breeze blowing at your back. Everything seems so quiet, so serene. Right?

Now all of a sudden . . . WOW! You jump right off the ledge and fly away! Imagine that you are Wonderwoman or Superman, and you can fly anywhere you want. So you fly off first in this direction and then in that direction, and even hover over the Empire State Building for a while. Eventually you land right in the middle of Central Park, full of excitement and bristling with energy.

OK, *open your eyes.* Isn't it amazing? Just as our imagination can immobilize us, it can also free us to do things we never thought we could do! **When we see ourselves achieving a goal—ANY GOAL—in our imagination often enough, we begin to believe that we can achieve it in real life.** We don't have to rely solely on our past experiences to determine our level of self-esteem. We can add as many new successes as we want—by imagining them over and over again in our mind!

Mohammed Ali once made this interesting comment: "The person who has no imagination can't get off the ground. He has no wings. He cannot fly."

By using our imagination in a positive and purposeful way, we gain control over what we think about. Now WE are the programmer, WE are the designer, WE are the creative force behind the reality we create in our life!

THE ALPHA STATE

We can imagine anything we want at any time and at any place. We can be in the shower, in an airplane, or just dropping off to sleep. One way we can imagine things with greater impact and effect is to enter a lower state of consciousness, known as the alpha state.

The human brain is constantly generating a series of pulses of electrical energy that are indicative of its current level of activity. During the day, these pulses are usually quite rapid, between 13 and 30 cycles per second. These higher frequencies are called beta waves,

It is always prudent
to take action and test
your methodology. If it fails,
accept it and try again.
But above all else,
try again.

WALTER STAPLES

and are associated with being fully awake and mentally alert, for example when you are intently thinking, talking or listening to someone. They are the ones you are generating right now as you read this book (I hope!).

Other brain frequencies are much slower. Alpha waves, for example, range between eight and 13 cycles per second. They predominate when we are very relaxed or on the edge of sleep. In the alpha state, we are much more likely to be creative. We often have flashes of insight or inspiration that occur spontaneously, usually relating to something we have recently been thinking or wondering about. A third type of wave, theta, pulses between four and eight cycles per second. The slowest waves of all are delta waves, which predominate when we are in a very deep sleep.

In the relaxed alpha state, we have improved access to our Subconscious Mind. The path is not blocked by the Conscious Mind which is constantly thinking and making judgments about what is relevant and what is not. All of our usual concerns and preoccupations with everyday life are put aside, thereby freeing up more neural circuits for more creative pursuits.

The alpha state is experienced naturally just before falling asleep and just after waking up. These are ideal times to condition our mind. Another option available to us is to induce an alpha state by conscious effort at a suitable time during the day by practising progressive relaxation. There are several ways to achieve this lower state of awareness. All have the same objective: to completely relax both the mind and body until we are in a transformed state of consciousness.

One proven progressive relaxation technique involves the following guided imagery:

Sit in a comfortable chair in a quiet room. Allow your eyelids to gently close. Imagine you are in an elevator traveling slowly down a series of levels to a place of total peace and tranquillity. Begin to count from one to 10, and as you do, pay attention to the growing feeling of complete relaxation in your body.

In using your subconscious mind . . . infer no opponent . . . use no will-power . . . imagine the end. You will find your intellect trying to get in the way, but persist in maintaining a simple, child-like, miracle-making faith.

JOSEPH MURPHY
AUTHOR OF *THE POWER OF YOUR SUBCONSCIOUS MIND*

Count one. Feel relaxation beginning to spread all over your face. Your jaw, forehead and scalp are totally relaxed.

Count two. You are going down farther and becoming more relaxed.

Count three. Your neck, shoulders and back feel soft and supple.

Count four. Your arms, hands and wrists are more relaxed. Your breathing is deep, slow and easy.

Count five. The elevator is moving down . . . you are experiencing deeper relaxation. You feel calm, comfortable and at peace with the world.

Count six. Your stomach, buttocks and thighs are all relaxed. Tension is literally evaporating away from all your body parts and extremities.

Count seven. Your legs and feet, even the tips of your toes, are relaxed.

Count eight. You are drifting down, deeper and deeper, and getting closer to your special place. You feel calm all over.

Count nine. Almost there. Feel the freedom.

Count ten. You have arrived! You are in your special place. Enjoy the feeling of total peace and serenity.

Now you are in a very restful state. Let's do an exercise that assumes you want to be just plain, old happy!

With your eyes still closed, see yourself at a distance sitting in a high-backed chair about 25 feet away. You see yourself as you are looking out over the universe. You see this person, who is actually you, as totally relaxed, at peace with the world, as totally happy. Imagine for a moment some of the thoughts that are going through this person's mind. There are happy thoughts from the past about

Lord, make me an instrument of Your peace. Where there is hatred, let me sow love; where there is injury, pardon; where there is doubt, faith; where there is despair, hope; where there is darkness, light; and where there is sadness, joy.

SAINT FRANCIS OF ASSISI
ITALIAN FOUNDER
OF THE FRANCISCAN ORDER
(1182-1226)

joyful occasions, loving relationships and personal successes. There are also happy thoughts about the future that make this person feel warm, hopeful and secure. Happiness is everywhere in this person's life and it is multiplying.

Now walk over to this person, and enter its body and its mind—you literally merge with this person so that he or she and you are now one. Now YOU are looking out over the universe with this person's eyes, and you are seeing the same things and experiencing the same feelings that this person saw and felt. Now you too are in a happy, restful state—now you also feel warm, hopeful and secure. Peace, harmony and happiness are all around you. You are literally radiating happy thoughts and experiencing happy feelings. YOU ARE HAPPY! Open your eyes.

MEDITATION

Another way to come into contact with your inner consciousness, and the powers and wonders of Universal Mind, is to perform regular meditation. Consider the following exercise.

Find a quiet place. Close your eyes. Count from one to 10 to enter a state of deep relaxation. Be aware that you are concentrating only on what is going on in your mind. Sense the complete solitude as the physical world begins to retreat from around you and you enter the silent recesses of your mind. Finally, you are alone. To begin, just let your mind go wherever it wants to go. Do not direct it in any way. If a certain thought enters your consciousness and begins to take hold, simply let it go. You will soon see that you are looking out over a vast universe of infinite proportions, a sort of cosmic wonderland whose tranquillity is interrupted periodically by streaking comets, which are simply thoughts coming out of nowhere and heading your way. You notice this and marvel at it all, but you just let them pass by. None directly enter your consciousness. By focusing on the splendor of what is happening before your very eyes, you become aware of how you can rise above the noise, clutter and drudgery of the thoughts and happenings of everyday life. You need not be preoccupied by any particular thought. You can choose to be a neutral observer watching everything quietly from a distance, and picking and choosing at will what thoughts you want to think. Divorced from body,

*The greatest discovery
in one hundred years
is the discovery of the power of
the subconscious mind.*

WILLIAM JAMES
AMERICAN PSYCHOLOGIST
AND PHILOSOPHER
(1842-1910)

all thought and past remembrances, you exist as pure spirit. Here then is your True Self, free from the effects of all physical sounds and sensations. You know whatever you choose, you can have and whatever you reject, will never touch you. You need only observe and choose to create the exact reality you want. It's like playing an animated computer game in which you control all the activity and initiate all the action. You say to yourself, "Boy, this is a lot of fun!" And it truly is. But you know for sure there is one thing you cannot do— you cannot turn the machine off completely. The "game," after all, does have a mind of its own!

PHYSIOLOGY

4. In point 4, we explained how we could adopt a certain physiology to get a particular feeling we wanted. We all have a physiology for self-confidence, for example, in terms of body posture, facial features, muscle tone, breathing pattern and tone of voice. There are many occasions when we want to feel confident in our life. I'm sure you can think of some, like a new job interview or giving a speech. So let's all stand up and adopt our most confident physiology, and in the process trigger within ourselves feelings of total self-confidence.

Ask yourself: was there ever a time when you felt absolutely GREAT, absolutely EXCITED, absolutely EMPOWERED (G.E.E. for short)? Of course there was! So begin to repeat the same words, see the same pictures, and feel the same feelings you had when you felt this way.

Repeat—"I feel great, I feel excited, I feel empowered!" Pair off with a friend and repeat, "I feel great, I feel excited, I feel empowered!" Stand up straight, put your shoulders back, look the other person straight in the eye and say, "I feel great, I feel excited, I feel EMPOWERED!" Now . . . don't you?

LOOK FOR SMALL SUCCESSES

5. The root cause of low self-esteem is a deep sense of unworthiness, all of which is undeserved. Why, then, if we are deserving of being worthy, do most of us feel the very opposite? Many reasons.

When one door closes,
another opens;
but we often look so long and so
regretfully upon the closed door
that we do not see the one
which has opened for us.

ALEXANDER GRAHAM BELL
INVENTOR OF THE TELEPHONE
(1847-1922)

Feeling unworthy comes from a lack of fulfillment. Fulfillment comes from actively pursuing our dreams. How many of us are doing that? And why not? We are locked in our comfort zone! Some of us are caught up in being perfectionists. We believe we shouldn't make mistakes. Nonsense! We know failure is a vital and necessary part of the achievement process. As well, others depreciate themselves by discounting their past successes. Most of us do a multitude of good things every day. Yet we tend to overlook them or take them for granted. We choose to forget just how good we really are!

Let me ask—have you done any of these good things lately? Bathe. Brush your teeth. Smile at someone. Help another in need. Give a compliment. Encourage a loved one. Read a good book. Share a point of view. Start a new project. Finish an old one. Obey the stop signs on the way home. Watch a television documentary. Empathize with someone. Marvel at a tree. Give money to charity. Stay within the speed limit. Pay your taxes. Hug a friend.

Just where does all this "goodness" end? Really, you are a pretty decent human being after all! So give yourself the credit you rightfully deserve.

Unfortunately, most people cling to their basic beliefs for a lifetime. They "awfulize" much more than they "fantasize." They stay locked in a prison whose bars are made up of self-limiting beliefs. They're afraid to break out of their shell of complacency. They dread the prospect that only failure and disappointment will meet them at every turn. But clearly no one has to accept such a reality. It's all in how we choose to run and control our thought processes, how we condition and direct our mind to see things the way they can really be.

Life is short.
Live it up.

NIKITA KHRUSHCHEV
SOVIET STATESMAN
(1894-1971)

YOU HAVE TO SET YOURSELF ON F-I-R-E!

KIM WOO-CHOONG

Kim learned the meaning of sacrifice and hardship as a teenager in war-torn South Korea in the early 1950s. With his father a prisoner in the north and his older brothers in the army, Kim was responsible for feeding his mother and younger brothers by peddling newspapers in the local village. He had to sell at least 100 papers a day to afford even a small bowl of rice. On some days, especially during inclement weather, he wasn't successful.

But even in the face of starvation, Kim never stopped dreaming. He believes that people with dreams know no real poverty, that a person is as rich as the dreams he clings to. In 1968, with $10,000 in savings, he and four friends founded the Daewoo Industrial Company in a small rented room. In 1991, 24 years later, the Daewoo Group of 22 companies had sales of $25 billion and employed 80,000 people.

Kim attributes his incredible success to self-discipline, a preoccupation with becoming brighter, smarter and better as a business person, and simple hard work. He values time as his most precious commodity. For example, his company has a tradition of not holding business meetings during normal working hours. He himself often works from five in the morning to nine at night. He has never played golf or gone to a concert. He says he receives all of his joy and satisfaction from his work—achieving his goals, using his creativity, and accomplishing what he has set out to do. In his book *Every Street Is Paved With Gold,* a best seller in South Korea, Kim's preference for simplicity is deep and unabiding. He comments: "Overconsumption becomes a bad habit. People fall prey to the temptations of laziness and extravagance at the expense of diligence and frugality." His example and work ethics are credited with helping to bring his country out of poverty and into a position of prominence in South-East Asia.

You make a difference by giving something of yourself for the betterment of others. Kim has made a difference. He dared to dream big dreams, and in the process, he set himself on fire!

A gem cannot be polished without friction, nor a man perfected without trials.

CHINESE PROVERB

CHAPTER 9

Have a Dream Bigger Than You

*Life means to have something definite to do—a mission to fulfil
—and the measure in which we avoid setting our life to something
we make it empty. Human life, by its very nature,
has to be dedicated to something.*

—Jose Ortega y Gasset

Developing a Sense of Urgency

I believe what people lack most in their life is a vision of a compelling future, a burning desire that stirs their emotions, and gives meaning and direction to their very existence.

What if you were told—right now—that there was a 10,000 dollar bill taped to the underside of one of the chairs in your house? Would that be enough to excite you to take some action? Or what if you were told there were 50 gold bricks in a vault in a bank in downtown Tokyo right now, with your initials on them, estimated to be worth five million dollars, and that the first person who showed up with your initials could claim them, would you do something about it? With how much URGENCY? Would you start by taking lessons in Japanese? Or by checking with the airlines to see when the off-season rates start so you can buy a cheap ticket?

I like this comment by Marcus Aurelius: "Do not act as though you had 1,000 years to live." Many of us don't have a lot of time left to do "our thing," whatever our thing may be. So we need a goal in our life just as exciting as 50 gold bricks with our initials on them—waiting to be picked up! Then, and only then, will we develop a sense of urgency.

I think the late Michael Landon made a profound statement when he said, "Somebody should tell us, right at the start of our lives, that we are dying. Then we might live life to the limit, every minute of every day. *Do it!* I say. Whatever you want to do, do it NOW! There are only so many tomorrows."

*If a man
hasn't discovered something
that he will die for,
he isn't fit
to live.*

MARTIN LUTHER KING
AMERICAN CIVIL RIGHTS LEADER
(1929-1968)

If you want to get really excited about something in your life, ponder this question, first posed by Dr. Robert Schuller, which I consider to be one of the most important questions you could ask yourself:

What one great dream would I dream if I knew I could not fail?

Wonderful question, isn't it? It's because it removes from your main attention all prospect of failure. It allows you to focus only on what you really want to do and succeed at in a major way—your very own dream, with your very own initials on it. It sure opens up the mind to the possibilities!

Here are some interesting aspects about dreams:

1. You can find fulfillment by pursuing any one of your dreams. You don't have to pursue them all.
2. You don't have to actually achieve a dream in order to find fulfillment. You need only actively pursue it.
3. By living and pursuing your dream, you not only help yourself, but contribute to others and the world at large.

Here are three other important questions for your consideration:

Of all the activities you can think of, which one gives you the most satisfaction, the greatest sense of accomplishment, and the greatest feeling of importance?

Don't prejudge whether you think you could perform any particular activity well. JUST ASSUME you can do anything you want extremely well. Knowing you have total choice, and your abilities are unlimited, what activity absolutely turns you on?

If you knew you had only one year to live, how would you spend your time?

He who has
a why to live
can bear almost
any how.

FRIEDRICH NIETZSCHE
GERMAN PHILOSOPHER
(1844-1900)

Assume you are healthy and on full salary during this time. And you don't have to go to work, do any cooking or any tedious chores. Everything is taken care of and your time is totally yours to do with as you please. But you know that after 12 months, you are going to drop stone dead. So, what would you do?

What do you want to be remembered for when you are gone?

This is like writing your own epitaph . . . in granite! What would you write today that represents what you want to be remembered for when you're gone?

The Principle of Purpose

This brings us to the principle of purpose. We have seen that one of our chief aims in life is to feel fulfilled, to be happy, to have joy, satisfaction and excitement in our life. Nothing is as important in this regard as our level of self-esteem: how much we like, how much we love, and how much we value ourselves. The principle of self-love says that we must literally sparkle inside if we want to be vibrant and full of creative energy.

To have these positive, empowering feelings, we need to be in the active mode—we need to be thinking, dreaming and doing. And to achieve anything that is significant, we need a plan to follow. A builder with an office tower in mind has blueprints. A driver with a destination in mind has a road-map. A chef with a meal in mind follows a recipe. And as individuals aspiring to great accomplishment, we also need a plan, a detailed game plan for our life that represents our very essence, our heart and soul that defines our innermost hopes and aspirations. Remember the old saying—if you are failing to plan, you are planning to fail!

So let's go to work to see how you should proceed. A game plan has two main components: a primary central purpose for your life, and various supportive and complementary goals that are consistent with this purpose. To discover what central purpose might apply to you, you have to ask yourself the question: "Do I know where I'm going, and why?" Why do you do what you do, what do you stand for, what do you believe in? Why do you get up in the morning and engage in the activities you engage in? What are you prepared to

Destiny is not a matter of chance,
it is a matter of choice;
it is not a thing to be waited for,
it is a thing to be achieved.

WILLIAM JENNINGS BRYAN
AMERICAN STATESMAN, ORATOR
AND REFORMER
(1860-1925)

sacrifice for, even die for, if necessary to achieve what you want to achieve?

In other words, what are the principal values in your life? The fact is, your reasons for your goals are more important than your actual goals. People who are driven, who are committed to their goals and their life purpose, are clear why they have them. They have taken the time to sit down and think through key aspects of their life concerning who they are, what they want to do, and what contributions they want to make.

Without a clearly defined sense of purpose and without a set of compelling reasons for doing what you want to do, there is no way you can ever feel good about yourself. Without a vision, a dream that is bigger than you are, there is no chance you will achieve anything of any real significance. You cannot truly like yourself or feel good about yourself if your whole life is just drifting along and going nowhere. If you spend your time just getting through the day, going through the motions, with all your evenings and weekends filled with TV trivia and idle socializing, there can be no accomplishment, no satisfaction, and no joy.

We all need goals to tap into and release our full potential. And the bigger the goals, the more potential we can tap. Research shows that the primary reason why many people are unhappy and stressful, why they are argumentative and defensive, is because they lack meaning and purpose, and a sense of direction in their lives. They are BORED silly! In our society today, young people in particular are conditioned to a large extent to be entertained and amused by external stimuli—television, Nintendo games, and rock music. They react. Seldom do they act. Seldom do they think for themselves, entertain themselves, or use their imagination. Hence they have no feeling of control, no sense of direction, and no finish line to cross.

Setting goals and making plans for their accomplishment is one of the master skills in life. Accomplishment is not a function of intelligence, education or specialized training. It comes from holding in mind a clear, precise picture of your heart's desire. A person with

*Until thought
is linked to purpose,
there is no intelligent
accomplishment.*

JAMES ALLEN
AUTHOR OF *AS A MAN THINKETH*
(1849-1925)

a clear, focused goal will always outperform a person who has no goal at all. Only about five percent of the general population have goals and only about three percent have written them down. Clearly the vast majority of people have no hope of ever realizing their full potential.

People lack goals for many reasons. They may not realize that goals are essential if they're to have meaning and purpose in their life—they don't understand the role that goals play in the Universal Achievement Process; they may not believe in themselves and in their ability to achieve important goals; they may not have taken the time to think through what goals would be appropriate for them; or they may not be willing to do what has to be done—to pay the price—in order to achieve them.

The curious thing is, goals tend to define themselves once you have decided on your primary life purpose—on the big WHY behind your life. When you can stand up, tall and proud, and state clearly and precisely to the world what you stand for, the hidden prompters will literally rise up from your Subconscious Mind and bombard you with ideas and insights about what you should focus on and how you should spend your time.

Goal Congruence

Your values are critical in the context of the goals you decide on. Values are principles that reflect ideal moral standards by which individuals guide their thoughts and actions. They are beliefs that relate to various moral aspects of your life. Values define what you believe is right or wrong, good or bad, fair or unfair. Truth, duty, valor, justice, honesty, humility, fidelity, compassion, tolerance, integrity and love—these are but a few of the many moral judgments you have to consider, and decide whether to adopt and practice in your daily life.

The only time your goals will work is if they are consistent with your deepest values. This is known as goal congruence. You have to know what your values are before you can map out a game plan for your life. And you have to be demonstrating these values by your actions and not merely professing them by your words.

The return from your work
must be the satisfaction
which that work brings you
and the world's need of that work.
With this, life is Heaven, or as
near Heaven as you can get.

WILLIAM EDWARD BURGHARDT DUBOIS
AMERICAN HISTORIAN, EDUCATOR
AND NEGRO LEADER
(1868-1963)

Actions don't lie. If you don't know what your values are, you need only look at your actions to see what they are. Values add the necessary emotional dimension—the focus, commitment and energy—to your goals. Without consistency between the two, your intentions are in conflict. Your logic says do this, while your heart says it isn't important to you. As a result, you lack the intensity, your commitment falters, no progress is made and you begin to feel less worthy and less capable. You begin to esteem yourself less. You decide then and there that setting goals is a very risky business. For you have found that by setting them, your weaknesses are exposed, you become vulnerable, you fail, and you feel hurt and demoralized as a result. It all boils down to PAIN! And people avoid pain like the plague.

If you want to have high self-esteem, if you want to feel fulfilled and be happy, you have to know that the direction you have chosen for your life is consistent with the values you want to live by. If you see by your deeds and actions in the physical world that you are manifesting your spiritual beliefs, then you'll radiate an inner glow and have an inner sense of peace and contentment that we all desperately want. You feel productive and worthy when you have a target you're aiming at, and are making meaningful and visible progress toward its attainment. Each time you reach a milestone along the path to your goal, you get a boost in self-confidence, your self-esteem goes up, and you set off more invigorated and more committed to your task. Goals are liberating!—but they must be consistent with your basic values, and carefully planned and organized in a meaningful way.

Primary Life Purpose

Here is an exercise that is specifically designed to give you some insight into a purpose for your life—your Primary Life Purpose. This is like writing a mission statement for yourself. Some countries like the United States of America have them (the U.S. Constitution), some corporations like I.B.M. ("service is our business"), and so should you and I.

Your Primary Life Purpose represents what you stand for, why you believe you are on planet Earth. It is what looks back at you when you look in the mirror each morning. It represents your very essence, your self, your soul. It is the real you.

Far away, there in the sunshine,
are my highest aspirations.
I may not reach them,
but I can look up and see their beauty,
believe in them, and try to
follow where they lead.

LOUISA MAY ALCOTT
AMERICAN AUTHOR
(1832-1888)

You must be careful to distinguish between a "purpose" and a "goal." A purpose is an overall direction, and it remains constant for life. Your purpose is fulfilled each moment of your life. In fact, it should never die, although of course you will. You can set and achieve many goals, however. A goal is tangible. Together goals support a higher cause which is not tangible—your primary purpose in life.

A purpose is something that only you can discover all by yourself. It is a simple, positive statement of why you are here. It tells you at any given moment whether you are living your life according to your "purpose" or not. Your purpose is like your inner candle, the "light" you radiate and share with the outside world.

I like Helen Keller's comment: "If you're in the dark, light your candle from mine. It will bring you light, and it doesn't diminish mine in any way."

To determine your Primary Life Purpose, here is a technique based on an approach first developed by Vern Black, author of *Love Me, Love Myself*. Start by completing the following three sentences:

1. I'd like to live in a world full of . . . Name five things.
2. Things I'd like to do and contribute to others . . . Name five things.
3. The most positive characteristics that best describe me, or the way I want to be . . . Name five things.

Out of the five answers to each of the above questions, select the one that seems the best for you, and circle it. Now you have one answer to questions 1, 2 and 3. Next, write down the following sentence, and place your three answers in the appropriate blanks:

I AM ACHIEVING MY PRIMARY PURPOSE IN LIFE BY HELP-ING CREATE A WORLD FULL OF 1. _____ BY CONTRIBUTING 2. _____ , AND WHILE MANI-FESTING MY 3. _____.

*Far better it is
to dare mighty things,
to win glorious triumphs even
though checkered by failure,
than to rank with those poor
spirits who neither enjoy
nor suffer much
because they live in the grey
twilight that knows neither
victory nor defeat.*

THEODORE ROOSEVELT
26TH PRESIDENT OF THE U.S.
(1858-1919)

By way of example, here is my answer. "I am achieving my primary purpose in life by helping create a world full of **fulfillment** by contributing **insight and knowledge,** and while manifesting my **helpfulness** to as many people as I can."

A Comprehensive Goals Program

The Primary Life Purpose exercise has forced you to identify what values are important to you. Now you can begin to build a comprehensive "goals" program around your primary purpose in life. By doing it in this sequence, you are ensuring that your goals and values are congruent and mutually self-supporting, that they are in harmony with your deepest convictions.

You can have only one primary life purpose, but of course any number of major goals to support it.

So, what major goals might be appropriate for you? Remember—you can have anything you want if you hold the vision of it clearly in your mind and work progressively toward its attainment. Think through what goals are critical to achieving your Primary Life Purpose. Here are three suggestions that undoubtedly apply to everyone: health, personal and professional business skills, and financial planning. With better health, we add to the quality of our life and the time available to us to complete our Primary Life Purpose. With better personal and professional business skills, we are more productive in our job and less likely to lose it. And through financial planning, we can better secure our financial future through proper management of our savings and investments.

Health

Our health is a function of many factors, some of which we can influence and others that we cannot. Generally there is nothing we can do about our genetic heritage other than be aware of any trends

Thought is first cause.
Believing in what you're doing
is second. The third is ACTION—*doing*
what you want to do, and
knowing you will succeed.

WALTER STAPLES

in our family background that might suggest we should take certain precautions. So what can we influence? Diet and exercise are a good place to start. There is undisputable evidence that poor diet is a major contributor to such ailments as heart disease and cancer. And we know that regular exercise has positive effects on our body in general and our cardiovascular system in particular.

So your goals could include any or all of the following: losing a certain amount of weight by a certain time; reducing your daily consumption of known undesirable products such as red meat, dairy products, caffeine, salt and sugar; lowering your cholesterol level by a certain percentage; designing and committing to a regular exercise program that meets your needs and suits your particular interests.

Personal and Professional Business Skills

We could all improve our basic skills, many of which we have never been properly trained to do. Writing and listening skills, time management, computer skills, parenting and interpersonal skills, presentation skills and speed-reading—all would add to our personal effectiveness and self-confidence. Learn as much as you can about your chosen profession—strive for excellence. Read all the books you can find on how you can improve the quality and quantity of your work. As well, people are increasingly being asked to speak in public, either for community or business reasons. Impressions are very important, and few things make a greater impression at the office than being able to talk confidently and persuasively at meetings and social gatherings.

Your goals in this area could include a commitment to take at least one course or seminar a month, read appropriate books at least one hour a day, and learn the basics of public speaking. You could then decide to give a certain number of speeches a year to volunteer or service clubs in your community as one way to hone and fine-tune your skills, as well as to make a useful contribution.

Financial Planning

People fall into three distinct categories with respect to personal finances. Either they are (1) in a deficit position—in debt, or (2)

First, have a definite,
clear, practical ideal—
a goal, an objective.
Second, have the necessary
means to achieve your ends—
wisdom, money,
materials and methods.
Third, adjust all your means
to that end.

ARISTOTLE
GREEK PHILOSOPHER
(384-322 B.C.)

debt-free—breaking even, or (3) in surplus—at least temporarily. It would seem logical that in order to get ahead, people who are in debt or just breaking even should strive to earn more money. But this usually doesn't work. People in these positions are in the habit of spending either all they make or more than they make. It follows that making more money would not improve their financial situation at all because, without breaking their current habit, the same spending pattern will continue.

Benjamin Franklin offered this sage advice regarding personal finances. "There are two ways of being happy: we may either diminish our wants or augment our means—either will do—the result is the same; and it is for each man to decide for himself, and do that which happens to be easiest. But if you are wise, you will do both at the same time." In short, he recommends both spending less and making more. Easy? No. Practical? Yes.

The average American earns over half a million dollars during a working life-time, yet only one in 100 becomes financially independent. And rare indeed are employees who can afford to miss two or three paydays in a row if they're laid off their job. It has been said that it isn't so important what amount of money you earn—it is WHAT YOU DO WITH WHAT YOU EARN. The truth in this statement is obvious but seldom taken seriously.

The advice: don't spend all or more than you make. Better yet, spend less than you make, say a maximum of 70 percent of your net salary, and invest the rest for long-term growth. You could put 10 percent into savings, invest 10 percent, and donate 10 percent to charity, for example. (Yes, charitable donations are a wise investment!)

Regarding savings and investments, you should take advantage of a phenomenon called compound interest that you first learned about in elementary school. David Chilton in his best-selling book *The Wealthy Barber* gives several great examples how it works.

Assume that when you were 18 years old you began to invest one dollar a day, or 30 dollars a month, at 15 percent interest. You are now 65. Your total investment has been $17,155. But guess what your

*The method of the enterprising
is to plan with audacity,
and execute with vigor;
to sketch out
a map of possibilities;
and then to treat them
as probabilities.*

CHRISTIAN N. BOVEE
AMERICAN HISTORIAN
(1820-1904)

investment is now worth—a cool $2.67 million! You may think that 15 percent interest is not achievable, but some mutual funds have shown consistent growth at this or even a higher rate.

Another of his examples. Consider amortization of a mortgage on a home, which takes advantage of compound interest in reverse. At 12 percent, a $70,000 mortgage costs $722 a month. The same mortgage, amortized over 15 years, costs $827 a month. By paying an extra $105 a month, you save 10 years of payments and a whopping $129,960! Of course the savings are less at lower interest rates but still are very significant.

David Chilton's entertaining and informative book gives many other excellent examples. It is must-reading. The point is, learn as much as you can about financial planning and the incredible effect of compound interest. Talk to experts in the field. But do all this when you're still relatively young—compound interest needs TIME to compound.

Formulating a Plan

To begin preparation of your comprehensive goals program, first write down all your goals on a piece of paper and organize them in their proper order of priority. For example, you should have at least one goal for each of the six key areas of your life. Next, select one major goal to focus on initially. Finally, outline a detailed plan of action for its accomplishment by following these specific steps:

1. Make sure the goal you select is meaningful, measurable and achievable. Choose one that is just out of sight but not out of reach.

2. Specify the exact date by which you want to achieve your goal.

3. Identify and explore various options that alone or together will enable you to reach your goal. Be creative. Don't just look at the traditional ways that first come to mind.

If you want to win anything—
a race, your self, your life—
you have to go
a little berserk.

GEORGE SHEEHAN
AMERICAN AUTHOR

4. Determine what actions you'll have to take to (a) acquire the knowledge you'll need, (b) develop the skills you must have, and (c) meet the people you'll need to know to assist you and give you the necessary advice.

5. Compile a list of the major obstacles you'll have to overcome to reach your goal. Determine how to deal with each one.

6. Compile a list of the major benefits, both emotional and material, that you'll receive when you complete your goal on time.

7. Once you have completed parts 1 to 6, write them all down to form a master plan. Understand that this plan is only a starting point, and will need updating and reworking as you take action and become more knowledgeable.

8. Begin to implement your plan at once, whether you think you're ready or not. If you wait until you know everything, you'll never get started!

Commit to do something every day that moves you closer to your major goal. The surest way to overcome fear, doubt and lack of self-confidence is to see yourself making regular daily progress. A walk of a thousand miles begins with a single step. And each step brings its own rewards. Success comes from experiencing success, from seeing it materialize before your very eyes.

Take 15 minutes twice a day, and read your master plan out loud to yourself. Best times include first thing in the morning and again just before retiring at night. As you read your goal, believe, see and feel yourself as already having achieved it in your mind. Bask in the positive feelings all this generates. By affirming, visualizing and emotionalizing your goal in this powerful and purposeful way, you are driving it deep into your subconscious reality.

Emotion Versus Logic

At this point, let's revisit the pleasure-pain principle to better understand how we can use it to our advantage to reach specific goals we have set. Why? We know people do things in life to either gain

*I always wanted to
be somebody,
but I should have been
more specific.*

LILY TOMLIN
AMERICAN COMEDIAN

pleasure or avoid pain. And this *emotional* aspect always takes precedence over *logic* in any given situation, and thus prevents us from taking the action we know we should.

Consider life-style choices such as wanting to lose weight, stop smoking, or eliminate chocolate or junk food from our diet. Logic tells us that such changes generally will improve our health and prospects for longevity. So why don't more people follow such advice? Simple enough: **they perceive more pleasure than pain in continuing their current behavior.** For our purposes, we'll look at financial planning as our example. Again, logic tells us that taking charge of our financial future is a necessary and wise thing to do. So why is it that so many of us put off taking any meaningful action— we procrastinate—thinking that time is on our side, and we'll get around to it eventually?

Again, the answer lies in our evaluation of ensuing pleasure or pain. Many of us see more risk than benefit in taking action in this scenario: "I'm not worthy; I might fail; I don't want to appear greedy; it's too much work," we say. The positives—more freedom, more security and more prestige—don't "weigh" as much on our balance scale. Therefore, again, emotion triumphs over logic and we do nothing. Yet, around age 45 or 50, we may not assess the situation in exactly the same way. We may meet some people in their sixties who are hurting financially, and conclude that NOT taking action represents more pain than finally beginning to start. On the other hand, we may also meet other people who took the appropriate steps early enough in their life such that today they are financially independent, and extremely proud of it. In the process, we have simply changed our idea about the amount of pain or pleasure we attach to specific behaviors.

Herein lies a clue—what I call the "push-pull" imaging technique—to how we can gain more control over the things we want to do or change in our life. First, we need to link massive PLEASURE to DOING what we want to do on the one hand—and let this "picture" pull us in this direction; and second, link massive PAIN to NOT DOING what we want to do on the other hand—and let this "picture" push us in the same direction. Easy to do? Well, we often do it

*Until you perceive
your own true worth as a person,
you cannot come close to
achieving total self-confidence.
Only to the degree that you truly
acknowledge your own unique importance
will you be able to free yourself
from self-imposed limitations.*

DR. ROBERT ANTHONY
FROM *TOTAL SELF-CONFIDENCE*

because of new information we acquire or new circumstances that arise by chance. So why shouldn't we do it because of choice? Our challenge now is simply to create the appropriate *pictures!*

Here is one way to link MASSIVE pain to doing nothing regarding financial planning. We know that government at all levels in this country (and most others) has increased taxes to outrageously high levels in the past 10 years. And this trend is likely to continue. In the process, it has robbed many people of a bright financial future. In my opinion, one that many share, government is big, powerful, greedy and wasteful. It always takes what it wants to quell its appetite by simply passing a new tax law. The onus, then, is on us to protect ourselves from this hungry beast the best way we can. This means getting organized, gathering information, making investment decisions and taking some risk. The alternative is to be consumed in whole or in part—by default!

You may recall the late actor Peter Finch's furious, cathartic exhortation in the 1976 movie *Network* that has achieved permanent status as a battle cry in American culture: "I'm mad as hell, and I'm not going to take it anymore!" Well, aren't you beginning to feel the same way? If so, think of this statement—better yet, FEEL IT all through your body!—every time you consider the current state of your financial affairs . . . and fight back the best way you know how: start taking some serious, purposeful action!

Flights of Fantasy

What flights of fantasy could help you achieve your goals? What would your life be like if you had already achieved all your major goals, and each and every day you were "on purpose"? Let's assume that one of your major goals in life is to be financially independent— a millionaire. As an exercise, close your eyes and see yourself as a millionaire. See yourself talking as a millionaire would talk, see yourself dressed as a millionaire would dress, see yourself walking as a millionaire would walk, see yourself thinking and acting as a millionaire would think and act in every aspect of your daily life. Now—how does it feel to actually be a millionaire?

*This is the true joy in life,
the being used for a
purpose recognized by
yourself as a mighty one;
the being thoroughly worn
out before you are thrown
on the scrap heap; the
being a force of nature
instead of a feverish
selfish little clod of
ailments and grievances
complaining that the world
will not devote itself
to making you happy.*

GEORGE BERNARD SHAW
IRISH DRAMATIST AND CRITIC
(1856-1950)

Open your eyes. If it's something that really turns you on, then it's probably something you really want. So "act the part" in every way with those you are with for the rest of the day . . . the rest of the week . . . the rest of your life! For a while, you'll feel uncomfortable. After a while, you won't. Such creative visualization gives you an exciting new picture and exciting new feelings about what you can be, do and have! Or you may want to ask yourself, "How would I spend a perfect day?" Ponder this question over in your mind. At what time would you get up in the morning? Where would you be living? What part of the country? What country? What kind of home would you have? What kind of car would you drive? What food would you eat? With whom would you spend most of your time? Would you exercise? How often? And on and on.

Consider what a burning desire could do for you. A burning desire would force you to pull together all your talents, all your abilities and all your energy, and focus them down a narrow path like a beam of light. As a child, I'm sure you've seen the power of sunlight when it's focused by a magnifying glass on a piece of paper or on the palm of your hand. Normal sunlight will never burn a hole through your hand. But focused sunlight will. And that's what a goal is—it's focused energy!

Life Is Like a Poker Game

We all need a big, challenging goal to provide meaning and purpose to our life. It gives us something to aim at, to work toward and look forward to.

A goal is a target to shoot at. If we don't have a target to shoot at, how can we score any points? And if we can't score any points, how can we measure any progress? And if we can't measure any progress, how can we get excited about any aspect of our life? We have to find a way to put some points up on our own scoreboard.

Life is like a poker game. Our ability to play the game is directly related to the number of poker chips we have in our pile. If we have only three chips, and everyone else around us has 100, guess who has the ability to take more risk? The universe rewards action, and action requires taking risks. We have to have sufficient self-esteem— enough poker chips—to break out of our comfort zone. Have you

*Ours is a world where people
don't know what they want,
and are willing to go
through hell to get it.*

DON MARQUIS
AMERICAN HUMORIST AND JOURNALIST
(1878-1937)

noticed that we are a nation of cheerleaders? But we're always cheering for someone else! We don't give enough thought to scoring points for ourselves. We don't purposely go about adding to our own pile of poker chips.

Take a hockey game. There are five players on each team gliding around on narrow steel blades, and each one is carrying a long wooden stick that he uses to whack his opponents, often over the head. All the players are covered from head to toe in heavy padding so that no one, not even their mothers, can recognize them. The objective seems to be to knock everyone down on the opposite team, then use every means possible to get this little black object—called a puck—into the other team's net. Each net is guarded by a guy who's got an even bigger stick, and wears a mask that's all painted up to scare away any unwanted intruders.

Every once in a while, someone manages to shoot the puck into the opponent's net, and instantly all of us in the crowd go wild. We yell, we scream and we whistle! But with all the padding that each player is wearing, none of us even knows who scored the goal! Meanwhile, all the players on the successful team mill around and pat each other on the back. They spend several minutes basking in their miraculous accomplishment.

At the end of the game, players from both teams are whisked off in their limousines to celebrate into the wee hours of the night. And what happens to us poor schmucks in the crowd, who actually PAID to come and see these guys play? We have to elbow our way down the stairwells, try to find our cars in a sea of vehicles, hope it starts, then spend the next hour or so trying to get out of the parking lot. A great way to spend our free time, right?

We have to wonder: have we got our priorities straight? We need to start putting some points up on our own scoreboard, and spend less time cheering for other people who are only getting rich at our expense. And NOW is the perfect time to get started!

*Man's mind,
stretched to a new idea,
never goes back to its
original dimension.*

OLIVER WENDELL HOLMES
AMERICAN WRITER
(1809-1894)

YOU HAVE TO SET YOURSELF ON F-I-R-E!

TERRY FOX

Terry Fox was born in 1958 in New Westminster, British Columbia, Canada. In high school, he showed remarkable athletic ability at a variety of sports. In 1977, when he was 19, however, tragedy struck. Due to cancer, Terry's right leg had to be amputated just above the knee. In time, he learned to walk, even jog, with a prosthesis.

Almost three years later, Terry had a fascinating idea. He wanted to run from coast to coast across Canada to raise $25 million for cancer research, one dollar for each Canadian citizen. Although many of his friends tried to discourage him, Terry couldn't be swayed. This was his great dream, his magnificent obsession. After extensive training, he set out from Cape Spear, Newfoundland, on April 12, 1980. For the next five months, Terry's "Marathon of Hope" captivated the imagination of the whole country.

But it was not to be. After running a total of 3,331 miles, an average of almost 24 miles a day, he had to stop due to shortness of breath. It was then discovered that cancer had spread to his lungs. He had gotten a little more than half way across Canada to Thunder Bay, Ontario. But was his dream in vain?

No. Within three weeks of having to stop his attempt to cross the country, Canadians were so moved by his courage and determination that they contributed $25 million to his cause. Although Terry died a short 10 months later, his dream lives on to this day. Every year, the "Terry Fox Run" is held in several cities literally around the world, and has raised to date well over $250 million for cancer research.

You make a difference by giving something of yourself for the betterment of others. Terry Fox has made a difference. He dared to dream big dreams, and in the process, he set himself on fire!

Life
is either
a daring adventure,
or nothing.

HELEN KELLER
AMERICAN WRITER AND LECTURE
(1880-1968)

CHAPTER 10

The Five Great Wonders
of the Mind

Success is neither magical nor mysterious. Success is the natural
consequence of constantly applying basic fundamentals.
—Jim Rohn

The Story of Markita Andrews

The ideas we have discussed so far can be described as a natural
cause-and-effect relationship:

When we change our . . . thinking,
(about who we are and what we can accomplish)
we change our beliefs;
When we change our beliefs,
we change our expectations;
When we change our expectations,
we change our *attitude.*

In turn,

When we change our attitude,
(how we act, feel and think)
we change our behavior;
When we change our behavior,
we change our performance;
When we change our performance,
we change our . . . life.

It's really this simple . . . when we change our THINKING, we change
our LIFE!

This is a story about a little girl, Markita Andrews, a true believer
who is a living testament to this very statement. Markita was living in
difficult circumstances in New York City. Her father had abandoned
the family, and her mother was forced to work as a waitress to support them both.

*Since the mind is
a specific biocomputer,
it needs specific instructions
and directions.
The reason most people
never reach their goals is
that they don't define them,
learn about them, or
ever seriously consider them
as believable or achievable.
Winners can tell you
where they are going,
what they plan to do
along the way,
and who will be sharing the
adventure with them.*

DENIS WAITLEY
AUTHOR OF *THE PSYCHOLOGY OF WINNING*

One day her mother confided in Markita and said she was saving as much money as she could to send Markita to college. Markita knew her mother had another dream—to travel around the world! Her mother had been saving travel posters for as long as Markita could remember. It seemed to Markita that her mother was giving up her own dream to help her get a good education. She knew her mother could never save enough money for both dreams.

Now, most children would probably leave it at that, believing there was little or nothing they could do to help. But not Markita. She began to think about what she could do. There didn't seem to be many options. As a student, she had to attend school during the day. And she was too young to apply for a job. But Markita was a Girl Scout, and one day her Scout Leader announced a contest selling Girl Scout cookies. The girl selling the most in her troop would win a free trip to summer camp. The girl selling the most cookies nationally would win a free trip around the world—for two!

Was Markita excited about selling Girl Guide cookies? Well, not really. Was she excited about winning the trip for her and her mom around the world? She sure was! (The goal wasn't as important as the "why" behind it.)

So Markita wrote down that she would sell more Girl Guide cookies than anyone else. She visualized her goal clearly in her mind— what she would do and how she would feel as she began to succeed. She then affirmed it in front of her aunt, who gave her this advice: "Go where the people with money are and ask them to buy cookies." (Sound like a recipe for success to you?)

So every day after school, week in and week out, from 4:30 to 6:30, Markita visited tenement buildings and shopping malls, and stood on busy street corners, confidently approaching prospective buyers. Politely and with a warm smile on her face, she would say, "I'm earning a trip to camp. Would you like to invest in a dozen Girl Scout cookies or two dozen?" She asked the same question over and over again, never doubting that she would reach her goal. And what do you think was the result? She and her mother went on that world trip!

*The secret
of success is constancy
of purpose.*

BENJAMIN DISRAELI
FORMER PRIME MINISTER OF ENGLAND
(1804-1881)

After five years of selling, she had sold 39,000 boxes of cookies! In the process, she also became famous. IBM invited her to address their salespeople. Walt Disney Productions made a movie about her called *The Cookie Kid.* Her book, *How to Sell More Cookies, Condos, Cadillacs or Anything* became a national best seller. Not bad, for a little girl with a lot of desire coupled with firm belief that she could reach her goal by selling cookies.

Once she was asked to address 5,000 top life insurance agents at a major convention called the Million Dollar Round Table. At the end of her presentation, she looked out at the vast audience, smiled and said, "I'm earning a trip to camp again this summer. Would you like to invest in a dozen Girl Scout cookies or two dozen?" She sold— 5,000 boxes!

As this example amply demonstrates, you have to plant the seed of belief in your mind if you want it to blossom and grow in your life. To believe is *to see;* to see is *to do;* to do is *to have* consistent with the original belief.

The Five Cups of Life

Consider the following chart which I have titled The Five Cups Of Life that puts into context the importance of beliefs in relation to accomplishment:

*Here is the test
to find whether your mission
on earth is finished:
If you're alive, it isn't.*

RICHARD BACH
AUTHOR OF *JONATHAN LIVINGSTON SEAGULL*

THE FIVE CUPS OF LIFE

FIGURE 4

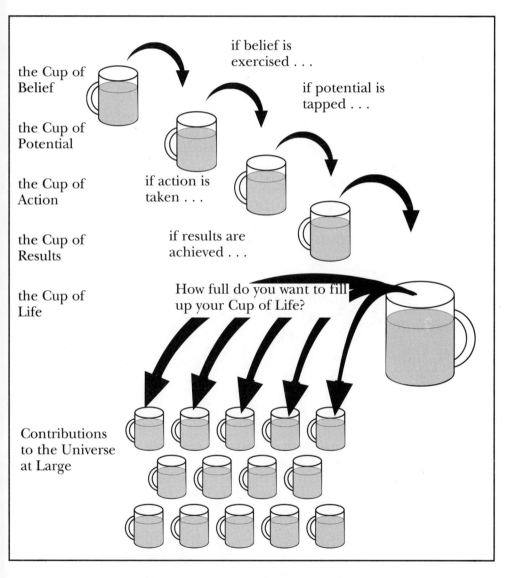

We are here to see what we can add to,
not to see what we can get from, Life.
—William Osler

*If one advances confidently
in the direction of his dreams,
and endeavors to live the life
which he has imagined, he
will meet with a success
unexpected in common hours.*

HENRY DAVID THOREAU
AMERICAN NATURALIST,
PHILOSOPHER AND WRITER
(1817-1862)

First, there is the Cup of Belief that flows into the Cup of Potential, that flows into the Cup of Action, that flows into the Cup of Results. The Cup of Results then flows into the Cup of Life.

But only if each cup is filled to its threshold can it fill up the next cup. If belief is not exercised, nothing happens; if potential is not tapped, nothing happens; if action is not taken, nothing happens; if results are not achieved, nothing happens. Your Cup of Life is filled only to the extent specific things happen in a specific way.

Now ask yourself: "How full do I want to fill my Cup of Life? Do I want my cup to runneth over so that I begin to fill up the cups of others all around me—the Universe at Large?"

So the starting point of all change and meaningful improvement begins when we change the most intimate beliefs we have about ourselves. Our mind doesn't know the difference between fact and fiction, hence we don't need to prove that what we believe accurately reflects reality. Remember, we create our own reality. We have to operate with a strong sense of faith that we already have the ability to do what we really want to do! Faith is a powerful force. **Faith is unquestionable belief.** It's the ability to see that which is not yet visible. It's not needing to have any evidence.

> You see things and you say, 'Why?'
> But I dream things that never were and I say, 'Why not?'
> —George Bernard Shaw

The brain operates very much like a computer. It accepts as fact whatever information we give it, and proceeds to act upon it. When given a goal we want and truly believe in, the mind begins to imagine ways to achieve it. When we give it a big enough "what" and "why," it takes over and starts to supply the "how" all by itself. We know our Subconscious Mind will take any **thought** that is combined with sincere **conviction,** and proceed to make it into *form.*

The Wonders of the Mind

The following points summarize many of our findings in this program. I call them the Five Great Wonders of the Mind:

He who knows not, and knows not that he knows not, is a fool. Shun him. He who knows not, and knows that he knows not, is simple. Teach him. He who knows, and knows not that he knows, is asleep. Wake him. He who knows, and knows that he knows, is wise. Follow him.

ARAB PROVERB

1. The first Great Wonder of the Mind. **We think in PICTURES, that are activated by words.**

This is how our mind actually works. We represent ideas in our head by way of PICTURES! Primitive humans communicated their ideas and experiences to others for thousands of years by drawing pictures in the sand or on the walls of their caves. Only relatively recently in historical terms have humans created various languages and alphabets to symbolize these "picture" messages.

PICTURES are things we put in our head. We think in pictures our every waking moment—we even dream in pictures at night.

EXAMPLES

Think of the word—WEDDING. What do you see? Do you "picture" the joy, the excitement, the beautiful bride, the happy faces of parents and giggling children? How do you feel? Think of the word—FUNERAL. What do you see? Do you "picture" the sadness, the sobbing, the sense of loss, the solemn faces of loved ones? How do you feel?

Or consider what pictures pop into your head when I ask you to recall—your first dance, your first date, your first kiss, your wedding night? (But please keep these to yourself!) Isn't it true, pictures always flash into our head when we hear a certain word? And various feelings and emotions always tag along to complete the picture. Note that the emotions we evoke are totally dependent on the particular pictures we have.

2. The second Great Wonder of the Mind. **We ALWAYS act out the pictures in our head.**

Notice that I didn't say sometimes, half the time, or whenever it suits us. I said ALWAYS! In fact, we "cannot not" act out the pictures in our head. The mind is a goal-seeking mechanism—it's called teleological. It takes a picture and transforms it into its physical counterpart, just like a Polaroid camera.

*We were deliberately designed
to learn by trial and error.
We're brought up unfortunately
to think that nobody should
make mistakes. Most children
get degeniused by the love and fear
of their parents—that they might
make a mistake. You uncover what is
when you get rid of what isn't.*

BUCKMINSTER FULLER
AMERICAN FUTURIST
(1895-1983)

CLICK! Act it out. CLICK! Act it out.

Let me ask: how do you see yourself at something you believe you are not very good at? Are the PICTURES and your PERFORMANCE exactly the same? Now compare this to how you see yourself at something you know you are very good at. Again, are the PICTURES and your PERFORMANCE exactly the same? Does this surprise you?

EXPLANATION: If you see yourself performing poorly, you'll tend to perform poorly. If you see yourself performing well, you'll tend to perform well. We always manifest in our behavior the pictures we hold foremost in our head. The result? Simply put, **we become in our life the person we see ourselves to be in our mind.**

> There is within us a power of complete liberation, descended there from whatever mind or intelligence lies behind creation, and through it we are capable of becoming anything and doing anything we can visualize. The mental stuff of which we are made is of such kind and quality that it responds to the formation of images within it by the creation of a counterpart that is discernable to the senses. Thus any picture we hold in our minds is bound to resolve in the material world. We cannot help ourselves in this. As long as we live and think, we will hold images in our minds, and these images develop into the things of our lives, and so long as we think a certain way we must live a certain way, and no amount of willing or wishing will change it, only the vision we carry within.
>
> —U. S. Andersen, *The Magic in Your Mind*

3. The third Great Wonder of the Mind. Here's the good news! **We can CHANGE THE PICTURES in our head to whatever we want!**

What is our most powerful tool? There is only one in our arsenal of weapons that makes us unique among all living creatures on the planet, that taps into our potential and determines the course our life takes. Any ideas? Yes!

*We tend to develop
a sentimental attachment
to whatever we are first exposed to
—whether the information
is right or wrong.
This applies equally to beliefs,
which helps explain why they
are so hard to change.*

WALTER STAPLES

It's our—**IMAGINATION!**

Our only true power lies in our ability to choose our thoughts. Imagination is the tool by which we can free ourselves from the bondage of the sensory world. You see, the world is a perfect place. It really is. It's only our thoughts by way of the pictures we form in our head that give it any meaning. There is no anger, fear, stress or disappointment in the world. There are only angry thoughts or fearful thoughts or stressful thoughts. And so it is—we control the pictures we put in our head, and thus create the world as we "know" and accept it to be. As Anatole France once said, "To know is nothing at all, to imagine is everything."

Our ability to use mental imagery has evolved over time to the point that we can form pictures in our mind in complete variance to the world around us. Let's see how easy it is to put pictures in our head. With your eyes open or closed . . .

IMAGINE! Can you see yourself—standing in front of the Statue of Liberty on Staten Island, looking up at the grand old lady as she holds the torch of freedom so high and so proud?

IMAGINE! Can you see yourself—driving across San Francisco's beautiful Golden Gate Bridge in a bright, red convertible, your hair flying about in the warm, summer air?

IMAGINE! Can you see yourself—in a sailboat in Jamaica's Montego Bay, skimming across the bluish-green water at 14 knots, the brilliant white sails stretching and billowing in the strong ocean breeze?

Now I want you to get *very excited* about what you just did. Because you just performed a series of miracles! You created pictures in your head of things you probably have never seen or done before. BUT YOU WERE THERE! You gave these pictures color, you gave them sound, you gave them meaning . . . in fact,

you gave them—**LIFE!**

*Ah, but a man's reach
should exceed his grasp,
or what's a heaven for?*

ROBERT BROWNING
ENGLISH POET
(1812-1889)

Now, can you see that if you change the pictures you put in your head, you change the way the world "looks" to you?

Let's demonstrate. See yourself

• making a perfect sales presentation to a new client, and closing the folder with the signed contract securely inside. How do you feel?

• performing superbly while responding to a series of questions during a new job interview, with all the interviewers nodding their heads in approval and agreeing with your answers. How do you feel?

• giving an inspiring, motivational speech to 300 sales professionals, and they all rise in unison to give you a standing ovation. How do you feel?

The trick is to keep clearly in mind the desired outcome you want. Your mind will then ensure that you act and perform in such a way that you will bring this picture into reality.

You see, we are the director, the producer, the scriptwriter and the principal actor on the stage of our life. To paraphrase William Shakespeare, "Life is but a stage, and we are all actors on it." We first create a sort of fiction in our imagination. **And fiction with sufficient fixity of thought becomes fact!** We have only to "see" it in our mind and follow it up with purposeful action if we want to make it happen in our life.

We always act out the pictures we put in our head. Remember we become what we think about. It's like flicking the channels on the internal television screen of our mind:

FLICK. Channel one. Old movie.

FLICK. Channel two. Horror story.

FLICK. Channel three. Negative pictures from the past.

FLICK. Channel four. Positive pictures from the past.

FLICK. Channel five. Aha! Finally. We see ourselves achieving our primary purpose in life. It's incredible. It's all so bright, in technicolor. It's full of sound and animation—it's seems so REAL! What

*If I had
to define Life
in a word, it would be:
Life is creation.*

CLAUDE BERNARD
FRENCH PHYSIOLOGIST
(1813-1878)

excitement! We rerun it a few times to get the PICTURE absolutely perfect. WOW! It's so clear. Isn't it interesting—the more clearly we see our future, the more control we have over it. Or is it . . . the more control it has over us?

There is no limit to our ability to think in PICTURES. We can imagine ourselves doing ANYTHING perfectly in our mind. And it is a miracle. There isn't a doctor or a psychologist anywhere on earth who knows how we do it. Remember that a picture imagined earnestly, vividly and in every detail in your mind can have 10 to 60 times more impact on the brain than a real-life experience. In other words, a picture we purposely create in our head BY CHOICE has the potential to be far more powerful than a picture from the outside world that is forced on us BY CHANCE! So who is in charge of your life? YOU ARE! But to be in charge, you have to take control!

The process of visualization is then perfected by taking repeated action until the desired physical results are consistent with the ingrained mental image. For example, you become an excellent public speaker by giving as many speeches as you can. Recall the Natural Success Formula we discussed earlier.

Previously, we also discussed another way we can organize pictures in our head—the way we "frame" them—to give us a different effect. Specifically, we can change either the CONTEXT of a given picture, or its CONTENT. Assume you see life as one big Nintendo war game. The following may be some of your impressions:

"Everyone is taking shots at me; things seem to be exploding all around me; I see things as big, bright, clearly defined and fast moving. It's all so . . .

One context you could adopt is:

CONTEXT 1—intimidating. The world is changing too fast. I am not sure how much of this I can take."

The very same impressions could lead you to adopt another context:

*Learning is not attained
by chance, it must be sought
for with ardor and attended to
with diligence.*

ABIGAIL ADAMS
WIFE OF JOHN ADAMS,
2ND U.S. PRESIDENT
(1744-1818)

CONTEXT 2—challenging. The world is an exciting place to live. Lots of fun, action, full of opportunities. I like it."

The first context could well be the reaction that older, less venturesome people would adopt, whereas the second may apply to more adventurous young people. Clearly the mental reactions—and hence the feelings—in each case would be significantly different.

As well, you could modify the CONTENT of the present picture to get any desired effect. For example, you could:

FREEZE THE FRAME. Note that everything comes to a complete halt. CUT THE SOUND. Now everything becomes quiet. BLUR THE PICTURE. Everything is fuzzy. Next, make everything black and white, and smaller and smaller, until all you see is a small black dot that slowly fades away and disappears into oblivion.

Clearly each of these mental adjustments changes the effect and impact of the vision. It's the way we organize what we see in our mind and the way we choose to interpret the things we see that determine their real meaning to us.

4. The fourth Great Wonder of the Mind. **The mind cannot tell the difference between fact and fiction.**

In other words, our mind doesn't know the difference between a picture we put in our mind *by choice*—versus one that gets there *by chance* . . . a classmate's rebuke, your father's put-down, or the "loser" label pinned on you by a close friend.

In light of this, you might think your mind is dumb, very dumb. Can you imagine a device as sophisticated as your brain not knowing the difference between fact and fiction? I can. A million-dollar computer doesn't know the difference between fact and fiction. It acts only on the information you give it—right or wrong, true or false, desirable or undesirable—then it provides the correct answer, not sometimes, not half the time, not only when it feels like it—but ALWAYS!

*Never judge
your potential
by what
your eyes can see,
but by what
your mind
can imagine.*

WALTER STAPLES

Assume that you want a computer to add 4 plus 4, but you type in 3 plus 4 by mistake. Guess what? You get 7 for an answer, right? But the computer did exactly what it was supposed to do—it added the two numbers given to it PERFECTLY. The computer is a perfect instrument. But it needs to be given the right data. And so it is with our mind. If we give it the right data—which is what? Yes!—the right PICTURES—it will always act out these pictures perfectly.

Imagine going to a movie. At the conscious level, we know the movie is just a movie, right? It's pure fiction. It's all staged and scripted. Actors and actresses are merely acting out roles assigned to them. But what does our Subconscious Mind do? IT ACCEPTS THE INFORMATION AS THOUGH IT WERE REAL! And because our mind can't distinguish between fact and fiction, our body reacts emotionally to all the scenes—we get excited, we become afraid, we laugh, we cry. It's all fantasy . . . but to our brain and nervous system, it's all very real.

Or imagine this scenario taking place in your life. You are driving along the highway. You've gone a few miles, perhaps driving a bit too fast and made "running" stops at two stop signs. Your seat belt is not fastened. All of a sudden, you notice in your rear-view mirror that a police car is quickly overtaking you, with its red and blue lights flashing on the roof. Let me ask you: what pictures begin to flash in your head? How do you feel? Are you a little tense? Nervous? Is your stomach starting to tie itself up in tight little knots?

Here is what happens. The driver of the car is Doug, your old high school buddy. He says he has tried to call you at home several times to ask—if you wanted to buy a ticket to the Policemen's Ball! Well, it wasn't what you thought it was, was it? Isn't it amazing how our imagination can mess us up if we allow it to?

Back to pictures. As an exciting new picture begins to turn into reality in your life, another miracle begins to unfold.

5. It's the fifth Great Wonder of the Mind. **The mind can imagine things for us that we cannot begin to contemplate.**

*Things won are
done; joy's soul lies
in the doing.*

WILLIAM SHAKESPEARE
ENGLISH POET AND DRAMATIST
(1564-1616)

Isn't this incredible? After you put the first picture in your head, your mind starts to put even more fantastic pictures there that normally you are not capable of doing. It's as though your mind is tapping into a source of knowledge or energy or intelligence that you consciously cannot. And of course, it is! Hidden prompters come out of nowhere, be they words or pictures or flashes of insight, and literally force you to think in new directions, to expand your horizons, to test your outer limits.

For example, if your goal is simply to get up in front of a small group and make a short presentation in a professional manner, your mind will help you do it. But it will also force you to consider speaking in front of 5,000 people, and literally sweep them off their feet! And it will proceed to bring into your life the people and the circumstances that will allow you to reach further than you ever thought possible, and in a way that you are not able to fully understand.

Colonel Sanders at age 65 could not have predicted that his recipe for chicken would result in a fast-food empire, with a Kentucky Fried Chicken outlet in every city in North America with a population over 30,000.

Or take Ray Kroc, founder of McDonalds. He couldn't have thought in his wildest dreams that his first hamburger outlet would eventually lead to well over 100 billion hamburgers being sold!

These gentlemen—excuse me, these RICH gentlemen—discovered a need in a changing society, and dramatically changed the eating habits of a nation, in fact of the world. (In 1992, after only 14 years in France, the culinary center of the world, McDonalds had the most sales of any restaurant chain in that country.) Now, you don't have to like the change and you don't have to be part of the change. But you cannot deny that a major change has taken place because of what they did.

It goes on and on. Whether a John Rockefeller, an Elvis Presley or a Mohammed Ali. They all started out with a little dream that grew

*If you always
major in minors,
you'll never make it
to the big leagues.*

WALTER STAPLES

larger and larger through hope and inspiration not all of their own making, which in turn led to fame and fortune beyond their wildest dreams.

Now, of these Five Great Wonders of the Mind, which one seems to you to be the most incredible of all? Hmmm. A tough question? After a little thought, I think you'll agree with me that it's . . . number 3: we can change the pictures in our mind to whatever we want. **Because it's the only one over which we have total control.** It means that we can imagine ourselves doing whatever we want in our life, and the Subconscious Mind automatically accepts the input as REAL, and begins to act on it to bring it into reality.

Few of us know what natural talents and abilities we actually have. They lie hidden, untested, waiting to show themselves. But to expose them, we need to replace our self-doubt with self-confidence, inaction with action, complacency with urgency. We can all excel at something, even achieve at genius levels—but it's up to each of us to take the initiative and find out what it is. There are opportunities all around us. Seize one that is of great interest to you, and see where it takes you!

𝕿he Sea of Galilee
and the Dead Sea
are made of the same water.
It flows down, clear and cool,
from the heights of Hermon
and the roots of the cedars of Lebanon.
The Sea of Galilee makes beauty of it,
for the Sea of Galilee has an outlet.
It gets to give. It gathers in its riches
that it may pour them out again
to fertilize the Jordan plain.
But the Dead Sea with the same water
makes horror. For the Dead Sea
has no outlet. It gets only to keep.

HARRY EMERSON FOSDICK
FROM *THE MEANING OF SERVICE*
(1878-1969)

YOU HAVE TO SET YOURSELF ON F-I-R-E!

JACK LALANNE

Jack LaLanne has a message we all need to heed: "Hey, take better care of yourself!" This from a man born in 1914, and who hasn't been sick since 1936—not even a headache! Jack's passion is good health and happy living, and he wishes it for everyone.

Long before Jane Fonda put on her first leotard, Jack was preaching the merits of exercise and good nutrition. As a reformed sugar-junkie, he built a backyard gym using weights made from cement poured into old paint cans. In 1936, he opened the first modern health spa in America. In the 1950s, Jack bounced across the TV screen, enticing millions of housewives to exercise. He made fitness trendy, and his show ran for more than 30 years.

Jack truly walks his talk. To celebrate turning 40, he swam the length of the Golden Gate bridge underwater wearing 140 pounds of gear. At 42, he set a world record—1,033 push-ups in twenty-three minutes. At 60, he frog-kicked from Alcatraz to Fisherman's Wharf, a distance of over 10 miles, handcuffed and shackled at the ankles while towing a 1,000 pound boat.

His day begins at 4 a.m. with a two-and-a-half hour exercise and swimming regimen. During the day, he manages his numerous enterprises—101 franchised health spas, and the Jack LaLanne line of nutrition products, exercise equipment, books and videos. Jack proclaims, "It's better to wear out than rust out. Most people don't die of old age—they die of neglect!"

Jacks summarizes his philosophy: "Anything is possible if you want it badly enough. I keep making new challenges and goals for myself—that's what keeps me going. With proper diet, exercise and attitude, you can live life to the fullest. So, don't make excuses. Get off your butt and out of your rut."

You make a difference by giving something of yourself for the betterment of others. Jack LaLanne has made a difference. He dared to dream big dreams, and in the process, he set himself on fire!

*The greatest use
of life is to spent it
for something that
will outlast it.*

WILLIAM JAMES
AMERICAN PSYCHOLOGIST
AND PHILOSOPHER
(1842-1910)

CHAPTER 11

Focus on Contribution

When we lose ourselves in giving, we find our reason for living.
—Anonymous

The Principle of Service

We have come all this way to realize one primary thing: that we begin to discover who we really are, our True Self, through the quality of the CONTRIBUTIONS we make. This is the principle of service, a concept so simple yet so profound. The Subconscious Mind is always creating to show more of itself. It creates by taking "truths" given to it by the Conscious Mind and transforming them into physical "things." Contributions are, by definition, offerings. And offerings are the things we give in order to receive. "As ye sow, so shall ye reap," it says in the Bible.

You may wonder what contributions qualify as being significant in the eyes of our Creator, thinking that small things surely would not matter. But you would be wrong, for the truth is, EVERYTHING COUNTS! Yes, everything. The mother who loves and protects her children, and creates a caring home environment. The father who works at his job to feed and clothe his family. The farmer who plants the seeds and grows the crops to feed people. The pastor who comforts and counsels, and spreads the word of God. The salesperson who meets the needs of people through the products and services he or she offers. All these things, all these services, are contributions first seen as pictures in the mind that are then manifested in reality.

All who serve, serve our Maker, for through their efforts, His work is done here on earth. The rewards are many. Some people, knowing they are needed and are making a difference, contribute solely for the emotional rewards. These rewards, though less tangible, are often the most meaningful and durable. What price can be put on such feelings as fulfillment, satisfaction, pride—in knowing we have loved, served, provided and cared. There is no price.

*The focus on
outward contribution is
the hallmark of
the effective human being.*

PETER DRUCKER
THE FATHER
OF AMERICAN MANAGEMENT

They also serve who contribute to the economic well-being of the towns and cities in which we live. Our modern social structure is characterized by almost complete interdependence, where we rely on each other for the many needs and comforts of life. Few of us are equipped to obtain the things we want and need without the use of money. Exchanging money for goods and services is a way of life. Our well-being, indeed our very survival, is dependent on it.

The principle of service may seem a bit too theoretical to some. You might say, "Nice words, but all simple platitudes. None of this is relevant to the real world." But, again, you would be wrong. The principle of service is basic to our modern capitalistic society. It can best be summarized by the statement, "Give, and you shall receive in kind." It's a reflection of the law of cause and effect—for every action, there is an equal and opposite reaction. When you get right down to the root meaning of success in business, it is simply to provide service. And the more service you provide, the more success you will have.

"To do more for the world than the world does for you, that is success," according to Henry Ford. That is quite a lofty statement from a famous capitalist. Yet he applied this very philosophy to his business, and gave it credit for the incredible success he attained in his life-time. The lasting wealth of this world is rightfully won by those who render quality service. And those who have surrounded themselves with a lasting prosperity cannot help but have enriched the whole world through their efforts.

To put all of this in perspective, let's look at the following schematic that I have titled The Contribution Matrix Chart.

*It is one of the most
beautiful compensations of this life
that no man can sincerely try to
help another without helping himself.*

RALPH WALDO EMERSON
AMERICAN ESSAYIST,
PHILOSOPHER AND POET
(1803-1882)

THE CONTRIBUTION MATRIX CHART

FIGURE 5

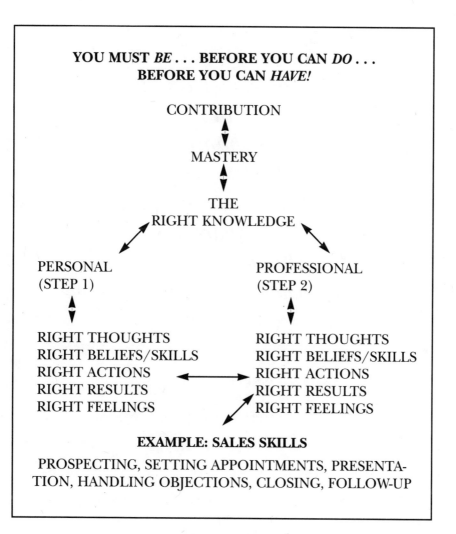

**YOU MUST *BE* . . . BEFORE YOU CAN *DO* . . .
BEFORE YOU CAN *HAVE!***

CONTRIBUTION

MASTERY

THE
RIGHT KNOWLEDGE

PERSONAL
(STEP 1)

PROFESSIONAL
(STEP 2)

RIGHT THOUGHTS
RIGHT BELIEFS/SKILLS
RIGHT ACTIONS
RIGHT RESULTS
RIGHT FEELINGS

RIGHT THOUGHTS
RIGHT BELIEFS/SKILLS
RIGHT ACTIONS
RIGHT RESULTS
RIGHT FEELINGS

EXAMPLE: SALES SKILLS

PROSPECTING, SETTING APPOINTMENTS, PRESENTA-
TION, HANDLING OBJECTIONS, CLOSING, FOLLOW-UP

Ask yourself:
"Is there anything I can't learn more about
in order to do it better?"

I don't like work—no man does—but I like what is in work— the chance to find yourself. Your own reality— for yourself, not for others— what no other man can ever know.

JOSEPH CONRAD
ENGLISH NOVELIST
(1857-1924)

It's relatively easy to get access to the RIGHT KNOWLEDGE to become excellent at our chosen profession: books, seminars, tape programs, articles, conversations and speeches by knowledgeable people. It is NOT as easy to acquire the RIGHT KNOWLEDGE to acquire the RIGHT BELIEFS about ourselves. **Yet it is these beliefs about ourselves that must be put in place before we can aggressively seek out, absorb and apply the RIGHT KNOWLEDGE about our profession.**

First and foremost, each of us is an individual who has acquired a host of beliefs, values and personality traits, all of which we carry around with us wherever we go. We bring OURSELVES to the office, to the meetings, to the family table. Hence it's critical that we have our act together, that we ensure we are pleasant, competent and productive people. We need to know who we are, where we're going and why, before we can be effective in any professional capacity.

We come back to an earlier point: we must BE in order to DO in order to HAVE; but many people want to HAVE in order to DO in order to BE. They set out to make money when in fact they should set out to provide service. It's so tempting to want money for the many things we know that money can buy: prestigious homes, luxury cars, expensive clothes, exotic trips, and the cottage in the country. So modern man asks, "How can I HAVE these things?" then quickly answers, "Money! I need to make money to have these things."

MAKE MONEY. The only one who literally "makes" money is the person who works in a mint operated by the government. The rest of us must EARN it. We earn it by providing others with goods and services they need and want. They do the same for us. The name of the game, then, is to exchange goods and services. And since it isn't always easy to pay for the car or home we want with the product or service we offer, money has been created to facilitate the exchange. Hence money represents nothing more than the value society places on various offerings, including our own. Its accumulation represents how well we are serving the needs of other people—customers, in competition with other suppliers.

The accumulation of money is a controversial subject for some people. They believe that to have just enough to get by is permissible, but to have a lot, at least more than most others, must be at the

*You can make your mind
a money magnet by running this
magnetic principle through the filaments
of your brain: look around you
and see in what way you can create
something that will benefit other people,
something that will help humanity
rise higher, suffer less, enjoy more,
become greater, achieve higher goals,
and then ask your subconscious mind
to guide you to the work that can
help you attain this magnetic goal.
When you discover what it is,
you can become rich and famous
through this magnetic discovery.*

NORVELL
FROM *THINK YOURSELF RICH*

expense of others. This is not the case. Money is simply a meaningful measurement of how well we are providing service, at meeting the needs of other people. We are willingly given money, and we willingly give it to others, all in the name of SERVICE. Of course, the more money we accumulate, the more we are able to contribute to the wealth of others because we can now afford to buy from them the things they offer and we want.

Those who pursue money as an end in and of itself are certain to be disappointed. For their focus is not on what they can offer, what they can give, or what they can contribute that meets the needs of others. It is on what they can GET by giving the least that meets their own selfish motives. All such people get their due in due course, as the law of mutual exchange is infallible. A person whose premise for success is founded on "taking" from others ends up taking only from himself. To get, you must give. Those who contribute to impoverishment must be impoverished in turn, and those who contribute to prosperity are themselves made prosperous.

For those who may doubt it, it does pay to "do good," both materially as well as emotionally. The research is irrefutable. Tom Peters and Robert Waterman state in their best-selling book *In Search of Excellence* that customer service, of eight key factors, was the critical one that accounted for the incredible success of the numerous firms they researched. Success in the marketplace is measured by the quality and quantity of the services that are rendered, and money is one of the main yardsticks for measuring this service.

Money, then, is never an end or even a means to an end. As a medium of exchange, it represents only service and is created through service. We cannot stop money from coming our way when we render service any more than we can we start it when we are not rendering service. Service is a function of our creativeness, our ingenuity, our willingness and ability to satisfy the wants and needs of other people.

Our capitalistic society operates under this simple tenet: find a need and fill it better than the competition. The result is goods and services being freely exchanged according to individual wants and

*I cannot believe
that the purpose of life
is merely to be happy.
I think the purpose of life is
to be useful, to be responsible,
to be honorable, to be compassionate.
It is, above all, to matter: to count,
to stand for something,
to have it made some difference
that you lived at all.*

LEO ROSTEN

needs. It is through the services we render that we live, and only by rendering service can we hope to prosper and grow. The system does place great demands on the participants—some would even say it's cruel. But it does provide the greatest rewards for the greatest number of people. As Winston Churchill noted, "The inherent vice of capitalism is the unequal sharing of blessings, whereas the inherent virtue of socialism is the equal sharing of miseries."

Consider how capitalism evolved into what it is today. In its most elementary stage, a person consumed exactly what he or she produced. The food you gathered, the clothes you wore and the weapons you fashioned all had to come from your own effort. As society matured, families began to produce items for trade with each other. You exchanged what others wanted in return for what you wanted. Clearly, the more you produced what others wanted, the more you could acquire what you wanted. You prospered as a direct result of your labor and ability to satisfy the needs and wants of other people in competition with others. This is the basis of our modern, free enterprise system. It doesn't mean you get anything free! Free enterprise means only that you are free to engage in enterprise.

In fact, we are all in business for ourselves, whether we realize it or not. Each of us is the president of our own personal services corporation, offering our services to the highest bidder. Regardless of whether we work for IBM, the government or ourselves, we are responsible for all the key aspects that are important to the success of any business: research and development; production; promotion; sales; and customer service. We in fact empower ourselves when we accept full responsibility for who we are both as individuals and professionals, and for the quality of the contributions we make.

The Principle of Excellence

After the principle of service, the principle of excellence most directly affects the quality of the contributions we make. Excellence represents a desire and commitment to aim high, to do our best at whatever task we are involved in. As John Gardner says in his book *Excellence,* "When we raise our sights, strive for excellence, dedicate

*In my wide association in life,
meeting with many and great men
in various parts of the world, I have
yet to find the man, however great
or exalted his station, who did not
do better work and put forth greater effort
under a spirit of approval than he would
ever do under a spirit of criticism.*

CHARLES SCHWAB
AMERICAN STEEL MANUFACTURER
(1862-1939)

ourselves to the highest goals of our society, we are enroling in an ancient and meaningful cause—the age-long struggle of humans to realize the best that is in them."

Excellence is a much used—and often over-used—term in today's business community. Public and private sector organizations are constantly trying to find new, innovative ways to foster excellence among their employees. Practices have included the carrot and stick approach of old to the newer total quality management (TQM) approach of empowerment from the bottom up. TQM, after all, is simply a process for marshalling the people resources of an organization toward valued goals and objectives. The challenge is always how to instill excellence in the INDIVIDUAL, since individuals and individuals alone do an organization make. Only to the extent that excellence is instilled in the efforts and activities of individual men and women is excellence instilled in the outputs and contributions of the organization as a whole, and in turn the market it serves.

The axiom of modern management is, "An organization is only as great as the people in it, and the people are only as great as the organization allows them to be."

Conceptually, there are only two ways excellence can be fostered and encouraged in an organization. The organization can attempt to impose it from the top down, by managers on down to individual workers; or it can be encouraged from the bottom up, by individuals at all levels agreeing to develop it themselves.

In most cases, individuals need only be given the climate, the encouragement and the tools to excel at anything. Individual creativity, insight, energy—indeed genius—can best be developed from within. Most individuals will readily accept the responsibility to develop themselves, to strive for excellence and peak performance, naturally, knowing that it gives them more freedom, greater control, meaning and a sense of purpose in their life. Initiative, dedication, loyalty and trust—these lie at the very root of excellence. And these personality traits and characteristics are best developed and sustained if they originate in the heart and soul of the individual. They cannot be imposed with any degree of effectiveness from without.

*There is no security
on this earth—
there is only
opportunity.*

DOUGLAS MACARTHUR
FAMOUS AMERICAN GENERAL
(1880-1964)

Hence the challenge for managers and TQM practitioners is not so much to define the various elements of the process that lead to excellence. It lies more in implementing the process cooperatively with people in light of their basic drives and motivations.

As individuals, we also have a choice. We can wait for the organization where we work to take the initiative, to begin the process in pursuit of excellence. But why should we wait and give up control? Besides, we could wait forever. We can decide ourselves to become excellent in our chosen field, and take the initiative to begin the process. No one else can do for us what we can do for ourselves.

Here are some interesting aspects about excellence. We find that many people go to work day after day, sometimes for their entire careers, and never think about becoming excellent at what they do. The thought just never seems to occur to them. And yet it is through doing something well that we generate positive feelings of high self-worth and high self-liking. This holds true in our homes, our schools, our institutions and our places of work. We all need little successes at conquering little challenges to spur us on to tackle even bigger tasks.

When I began my career as a writer and professional speaker, my life started to improve, opportunities came my way, and my income went up THE VERY INSTANT I decided that I was going to become excellent at what I did. I bought the books, I took the courses, I listened to the tapes, I sought advice from the experts—in short, I took the time and made the effort to learn everything I could about my craft.

The same holds true for any area of endeavor. If you study the lives of successful men and women in all walks of life—from politicians, inventors, scientists, academics, to business leaders and professional athletes—you'll find that every life begins to become great when you make the decision to become the best at what you do. Unless you make a conscious decision to become outstanding in your chosen field, by default you are agreeing to accept mediocrity as your standard.

*We are here on earth
to do good for others.
What the others are here for,
I don't know.*

WYSTAN HUGH AUDEN
ENGLISH POET IN THE U.S.
(1907-1973)

So what are some of the elements of a self-initiated and self-directed program to develop personal and professional excellence? Consider the following:

1. Develop an appreciation of what excellence is in the area in which you want to specialize.

Ask yourself, "What are the skills I need to develop that will equate to excellence in my particular field? Who are some role models in my field that I can study and emulate? What are some of the key result areas I should be aiming for that would equate to excellence?" In other words, you must have some conception of what excellence is before you can begin to pursue it and acquire it.

2. Understand that excellence is not a destination, it's a journey.

You never arrive at excellence. You pursue it all of your life. Some people naturally wonder why they should commit themselves to a goal that they will never reach. For many reasons. The rewards come from each step that is taken. And the rewards vastly outnumber and outweigh the amount of effort that has to be expended. You will never achieve anything significant unless you find out what it is you are good at. The alternative is to be condemned to doing a job in a mediocre and lacklustre way for eight or 10 hours a day for the rest of your life.

3. List the many benefits that will accrue to you as a result of becoming excellent in your career.

Benefits come in the form of emotional and material rewards. In both cases, the market only pays excellent rewards for excellent performance, average rewards for average performance, and below average rewards for below average performance. You can expect to get out of something only in proportion to what you put in.

Emotionally, you can never get excited or have any real joy or satisfaction from doing something in an average and mediocre way. You only feel truly great as a result of doing something in an outstanding and exemplary way. In fact, *all self-esteem is rooted in a feeling of mastery*

*People are always blaming
their circumstances
for what they are.
I don't believe in circumstances.
The people who get on in this world
are the people who get up and look for
the circumstances they want,
and, if they don't find them,
make them.*

GEORGE BERNARD SHAW
IRISH DRAMATIST AND CRITIC
(1856-1950)

and competence at something you feel is important. It is in knowing that you are capable and valued by others, and are making a meaningful contribution.

Financially, as well, peak performers are the biggest winners. In almost all competitive fields, a general rule seems to apply known as the 80/20 rule: the top 20 percent earn 80 percent of the income.

EXAMPLES

- the top 20 percent of salespeople earn 80 percent of the income;
- the top 20 percent of actors earn 80 percent of the income;
- the top 20 percent of authors earn 80 percent of the income;
- the top 20 percent of singers earn 80 percent of the income;
- the top 20 percent of professional athletes earn 80 percent of the income.

Whether you are an artist, an office worker, a teacher, a sales clerk, a salesperson, a secretary or a nurse, excellence pays!

4. List the things you need to do and the obstacles you must overcome in your quest to become excellent.

What people do you have to meet, what courses do you have to take, what books do you have to read, what skills do you have to develop, what effort do you have to expend, what time commitments do you have to make, what sacrifices do you have to endure, all in the name of personal excellence?

Thomas Huxley wrote, "Perhaps the most valuable result of all education is the ability to make yourself do the thing you have to do, when it ought to be done, whether you like it or not."

Some people will tell you that they did all the things they thought they should have done, and yet they were not successful. Then you must simply ask them, "What were the things you were NOT willing to do?" Invariably, there was at least one critical thing.

The day was dying, the night
being born—but with great peace.
Here were the imponderable processes
and forces of the cosmos, harmonious
and soundless. Harmony, that was it!
That was what came out of the silence—
a gentle rhythm, the strain of a perfect chord,
the music of the spheres, perhaps.
It was enough to catch that rhythm,
momentarily to be myself a part of it.
In that instant, I could feel no doubt
of man's oneness with the universe.
The conviction came that the rhythm
was too orderly, too harmonious, too perfect
to be a product of blind chance—that,
therefore, there must be purpose in the whole
and that man was part of that whole
and not an accidental offshoot.
It was a feeling that transcended reason;
that went to the heart of man's despair
and found it groundless. The universe
was a cosmos, not a chaos; man was
as rightfully part of that cosmos
as were the day and night.

RICHARD E. BYRD
AMERICAN NAVAL OFFICER, FLYER AND ARCTIC EXPLORER
(1888-1957)

5. Commit to these steps, no matter what, knowing that this is the price you have to pay to reap the rewards you want.

A commitment to excellence is a small price to pay for a life-time of joy and satisfaction. You cannot hide from the world. Change, challenges, difficulties—these will never go away. Nor should you want them to. What you need to do, however, is to rise up in spirit and temperament to meet them head on, to welcome them, indeed, to indulge in them. **Challenge life to challenge you!** In this way, you shall truly find what you are really made of.

We can never get more out of life than what we put in. But of course, there is no limit to what we can put in . . . in terms of time, effort, creativity and commitment. We need to be a constant giver to our world. We need forever to be looking for ways to make contributions that are important to ourselves and others, that add value to those in need around us and that by natural law, add value to us in return in the form of the many rewards that are sent our way, rewards that we can't turn off even if we wanted to.

The I.C.A.N. Principle™

In business, the Japanese have adopted a very simple yet effective approach to quality improvement—and excellence—in both product design and manufacturing methods. It was taught to them by the late Dr. W. Edwards Deming, the famous American quality control expert who helped the Japanese rebuild in the 1950s after the Second World War. The Japanese call this concept "kaizen," which literally means "constant improvement." The idea involves making small, simple changes on a continuous basis, over and over again, in pursuit of perfection. The Japanese understand that tiny refinements when coupled together lead ultimately to significant improvements, often to levels not previously considered possible. The goal is to bring about change in a gradual, evolutionary way rather than a rapid, revolutionary way.

Each of us can apply this very same concept to our own personal and professional development. After all, to succeed and be happy,

We must not cease from exploration.
And the end of all our exploring
will be to arrive where we began
and to know the place for the first time.

T. S. ELIOT
AMERICAN POET, CRITIC AND ESSAYIST
(1888-1965)

we have to be constantly growing, constantly improving our knowledge and skills in ceratin key areas. A few years ago, I created the acronym I.C.A.N. to teach this philosophy in my seminars, which follows from the phrase **I**mprovement that is **C**onstant **A**nd **N**ever-ending. Of course, I.C.A.N. also means "I can," an affirmation consistent with this fascinating concept. For we know that the only real joy in life comes from knowing we can and are improving ourselves in some significant way every day of our lives. This makes life a wondrous and exciting adventure, a journey in search of excellence . . . in search of our True Self.

Since there is no other way of doing it, constant improvement equates to constant learning. Learning as practiced in the last 100 years no longer has the same meaning. No longer is learning done only in schools, at a specific time in our life, and with a fixed methodology. Today's new economy dictates that learning means **lifelong learning**—the development of new skills, thought processes and greater creativity, and acquiring more knowledge about a wide variety of disciplines. I've heard it said—and I believe it to be true— that you can beat 45 percent of the competition through shear hard work, another 45 percent through constant learning, which leaves you in the top 10 percent. And to compete at this level is an all-out dog fight. But this is where you want to be to find out what you're really made of!

The Great Wheel of Life

At this point, let's review and put in perspective how we organize our time and focus our resources on a daily basis. We have already described the six key areas of our life, those aspects that when added together determine **the quality of life** that we enjoy.

The following depiction, which I call THE GREAT WHEEL OF LIFE, helps us conceptualize the notion that each of these six areas is like a spoke in a large wheel. Two facts are of note. First, the wheel is strong only if all six spokes are present and are significant players. Otherwise, if one or more spokes is missing, the wheel is distorted in shape and wobbles when put in motion. Like a car with a flat tire going down the road, you hear a loud whop! whop! whop! If the distortion is significant enough, the wheel even collapses. And so it can

*The spirit of self-help is
the root of all genuine
growth in the individual;
and, exhibited in the lives
of many, it constitutes the
true source of national
vigor and strength.
Help from without is often
enfeebling in its effects,
but help from within
invariably invigorates.*

SAMUAL SMILES
SCOTTISH-BORN AUTHOR
OF THE CLASSIC BOOK *SELF-HELP*
(1812-1904)

be with our life! Second, our very own sense of self lies at the core of the wheel, and directly affects all the other parts.

Real-life examples are everywhere. We know if we ignore our relationships, our life comes apart. The spiralling divorce rates are a prime example of personal tragedy, of couples and families being torn apart. And the devastating effects of excessive alcohol or drugs on our body are well known to us all. John Belushi, William Holden, Freddie Prinze, Elvis Presley, Janis Joplin, Jimi Hendrix . . . these are just some of the people we know who paid the ultimate price. As well, we don't want to work all our life, only to retire broke and dependent on social assistance. Hence we must engage in some meaningful financial planning.

The key, then, is to ensure that we are making constant improvements in each of these areas, and have a proper **balance** among all six areas such that each area is nurtured and enhanced. In this way, a synergetic effect is created and momentum generated. The goal is to have each individual area generate its own amount of joy and fulfillment, all contributing a significant part to the greater whole—a fulfilling, rewarding and meaningful life.

THE GREAT WHEEL OF LIFE

FIGURE 6

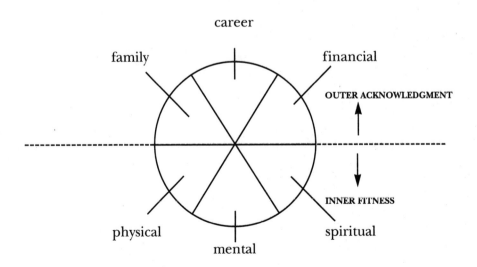

*It requires
a very unusual mind
to understand
the analysis
of the obvious.*

ALFRED NORTH WHITEHEAD
FROM *SCIENCE
AND THE MODERN WORLD*

I'd like to share with you this poem that I wrote. It is titled "The Secret of Living is Giving."

> I sit in solitude
> And contemplate life.
> I marvel at Nature,
> I cry at strife.
>
> I ask, "What can be done
> By only one mind?"
> The answer comes back—
> "A goal you must find!"
>
> So a goal I must find
> One bigger than me.
> I decide to give—thoughts,
> To help Humanity.
>
> It's hope I send out
> So that all can see,
> We are what we are
> But we can be what we can be.
>
> So—look up and look out,
> Give what you can give.
> It's your special blessing
> Helping others to live!

To conclude this chapter, I leave you with this thought from Philippians 1:6.

> "Be confident of this very thing, that He who
> has begun a great work in you will complete it."

*Someday, after we have mastered
the winds, the waves, the tide
and gravity, we shall harness for God
the energies of love.
Then, for the second time in the history
of the world, man will have discovered fire.*

PIERRE TEILHARD DE CHARDIN
JESUIT PHILOSOPHER
(1881-1955)

YOU HAVE TO SET YOURSELF ON F-I-R-E!

LILA AND DeWITT WALLACE

Lila asnd DeWitt Wallace were avid readers. While reading magazines, they often found articles they enjoyed and wanted to share with friends. They were always thinking of other people in their life, and about ways they could help them.

They discussed the subject often, and together decided on a novel idea: they would clip the very best articles they could find from other magazines, get permission to reprint abridged versions of them, and then put them together in a new magazine called *Reader's Service*.

Established publishers thought the Wallaces were crazy. "Why would anyone buy 'second-hand' articles?" they asked. Even the famous newspaper publisher William Randolph Hearst offered an opinion. He said their scheme wasn't economical, that it wouldn't sell the necessary 100,000 copies to break even.

But Lila and DeWitt believed in their idea and that it was a meaningful way they could help people. They began publishing their little magazine in Pleasantville, N.Y., in 1922. Today, *Reader's Digest* is published in 17 languages around the world. It has more than 16 million paid subscribers, and a readership that exceeds 100 million people worldwide.

You make a difference by giving something of yourself for the betterment of others. Lila and DeWitt Wallace have made a difference. They dared to dream big dreams, and in the process, they set themselves on fire!

*The future
belongs to those
who believe in
the beauty of their
dreams.*

ELEANOR ROOSEVELT
POLITICAL ACTIVIST
AND WIFE OF FRANKLIN DELANO ROOSEVELT
32ND U.S. PRESIDENT
(1884-1962)

CHAPTER 12

Exploring Our
Spiritual Dimension

*A psychological transformation is not possible without
a spiritual awakening, and before a man can change his kind
and type of thinking, it first is necessary that he alters
his conception of self.*

—U. S. Andersen

Assessing Our Results

So where do all the ideas presented so far take us? We have traveled down this road a long way. Now it's time to bring it all together to see if there is a central theme to life—how to live it to the fullest, how to make the greatest contribution—knowing that as human beings, we have many limitations and inherent deficiencies.

The following summarizes many of our key findings:

1. Human nature, if left unchecked, unchallenged and uncharted will destroy us all, one at a time. We can sink, simply survive or succeed according to our basic drives. We each have the means to fall to the depths of despair or rise to the heights of greatness.

2. Each of us develops a collective consciousness that is essentially our understanding of ourselves. It answers the question, "Who am I?" It represents our sense of self in relation to our world and what we see as our possibilities in it.

3. The human mind has a sort of "bifocal" sensing capability to understand itself and its world: we can look outward, and see what is there. This is usually our prime focus for the first part of our life. Or we can look inward, and see what might be there. We usually do this later in life. One or other perspective always predominates.

4. If our main focus is outward at the physical world, we will tend to see all the negatives that exist: violence, anger, greed, hatred, fear

*The mind of man
is capable of anything—
because everything is in it,
all the past as well as
all the future.*

JOSEPH CONRAD
ENGLISH NOVELIST
(1857-1924)

and corruption. If our focus is primarily inward, we will tend to see all the positives and possibilities inherent in our very nature: love, kindness, compassion, empathy and respect.

5. There is a universal intelligence all around us. It is everything, everywhere, in all things. It is infinite, all-knowing and all-powerful. Each of us can access this intelligence, since we are it and it is us.

6. We always see the world around us in relation to how we see ourselves. It is our beliefs, our knowledge, our understanding—our inner *consciousness*—through which we interpret events that happen or exist in our environment. Life as we know it is not a physical thing; **it is a mental construct.**

7. Each of us operates on the basis of our limited understanding of ourselves and our world. In this way, we create an Artificial Self that bears no relation to who we really are. Our True Self is who each of us in fact is. We represent universal intelligence accessible by one mind.

8. We have unlimited abilities to be, to do and to have. But it is only through our beliefs, our values and our actions that we achieve anything, and come to understand more about our true nature.

9. Our ability to contemplate, conceptualize, introspect and imagine are the tools we can use to discover who we really are. It is by first changing our inner world, how we see ourselves, that we change our outer world.

10. Our primary purpose in life is to discover who we really are, our True Self. We achieve this by making meaningful CONTRIBUTIONS, using all of our natural talents and abilities. It is to GIVE of ourselves. The skill that allows this to happen is mastery of ourselves—how we think and how we behave, which leads to mastery of life.

Mastery of life has as its very foundation knowledge and understanding—of ourselves and our world, of others, of our profession, of our primary purpose in life, of the cause behind all things.

*Public opinion
is a weak tyrant
compared with our own
private opinion.
What a man thinks of himself . . .
that is what determines
his fate.*

HENRY DAVID THOREAU
AMERICAN NATURALIST,
PHILOSOPHER AND WRITER
(1817-1862)

We come back to this simple truth: It matters not where we were born, who our parents were, what our level of education is, what language we speak, what skills we have developed, or what successes or failures we have had. IT MATTERS ONLY WHO WE THINK WE ARE!

The following statements may seem more of a puzzle than a great revelation, but they do illustrate the points we have made:

1. We think we know who we are.
2. We always act out who we think we are.
3. We are NOT who we think we are.
4. We will never know who we really are.

BUT

5. We can change who we think we are, and in the process,

WE CHANGE WHO WE ARE!

Thought is first cause. In the beginning, we are. Pure consciousness. As we are, we think. As we think, we believe. As we believe, we imagine. As we imagine, we become. As we become, we do. As we do, we contribute. As we contribute, we receive. As we receive, we become fulfilled. All in search of our True Self.

Our Individual Scorecard Says . . .

How well are you doing today? What does your scorecard say? Are you winning more than you're losing? Or is it the other way around? Is it possible to come to any meaningful conclusions in this regard? Well, most of us are asked the following question several times a day by others:

The strongest single factor in prosperity consciousness is self-esteem: believing you can do it, believing you deserve it, believing you will get it.

JERRY GILLIES
AUTHOR OF *MONEYLOVE*

"How are you doing?"

Of course, the question may be phrased a little different— "How are you? How are things? How is it going?"—but it's an interesting question nonetheless. It addresses the point of how well do we think we're doing in our life at the particular time we're asked. And since most of us usually have a lot on our mind at the time we're asked— we are supposedly preoccupied by more weighty concerns, like watching the numbers on the elevator wall flip by or wondering how long until lunch-time—we pay little attention and give little thought to our answer.

Herein lies the value and insight represented by our response. Since we don't give any serious conscious thought to our answer before we give it—it's spontaneous, a knee-jerk reaction, it's like we're in a trance—it comes straight from the Subconscious Mind. Hence it represents a great inner truth that often even we are not consciously aware of: do we think we're moving ahead, marking time, or simply going backward in the whole scheme of things? Do we feel we are indeed making progress toward a grander cause, that our life is indeed meaningful and fulfilling? Or are we like scraps of paper blowing in the wind, at one moment happy, the next moment sad, depending on whether the wind is blowing in a favorable direction?

Like the countenance on our face, the gleam in our eye or the briskness in our step, our everyday responses to this simple question are a window to our soul. We are indebted to Dr. Robert Schuller for the following insightful illustration that sheds some light on this not-at-all-simplistic phenomenon.

ROBERT SCHULLER'S SCALE OF THE HUMAN SPIRIT

Our collective consciousness exists and operates at many levels. But it is always there and always working. We can gain some insight into its current state and "status"—its relative vibrancy—if we listen to what we say to ourselves and to others. For example, here are 10

*During the past 30 years,
people from all the civilized countries
of the earth have consulted me.
Many hundreds of patients have passed
through my hands. Among all my patients
in the second half of life—that is to say,
over 35—there has not been one
whose problem in the last resort was not
that of finding a religious outlook on life.
It is safe to say that every one of them
fell ill because he had lost what the living
religions of every age have given
to their followers, and none of them
has been really healed who did not regain
his religious outlook.*

CARL JUNG
SWISS PSYCHOLOGIST
(1875-1961)

possible responses on a scale of one to 10 (lowest to the highest) that people often use to answer this question posed to them by others, usually several times a day:

"How are you doing?"

RANGE OF ANSWERS:

1. **No answer.** The person is in shock; overcome by grief or loss.

2. **"I'm MAD!"** The person is consumed by ANGER.

3. **"I'm depressed."** The person is being controlled by negative thoughts and feelings.

   despite good health, wealth, love, status and excellent future prospects

4. **"Not so bad."** The person is barely functioning; watching things happen.

5. **"I'm OK."** The person is coping, but very vulnerable.

6. **"I'm good."** The positives slightly outweigh the negatives.

7. **"I'm terrific!"** And still only at #7. An element of control.

   despite disease, decay, depression, despair or even imminent death

8. **"I'm fantastic!"** Greater control; potential for greater accomplishment.

9. **"I'm super!"** In control; making things happen.

10. **"I'm . . . simply sensational!"** In control. In charge. Incredible!

Every act rewards itself.
Cause and effect, means and ends,
seeds and fruit cannot be severed.
For the effect already blooms in the cause,
the end pre-exists in the means,
the fruit in the seed.

RALPH WALDO EMERSON
AMERICAN ESSAYIST,
PHILOSOPHER AND POET
(1803-1882)

Think for a moment about the typical answers you give on a daily basis. Do your answers ever go from one extreme to another, depending on your particular circumstances at a certain point in time? Or are they always the same, whatever your circumstances are? Give some serious thought to these questions.

This chart offers some interesting insights. Some people can be up, they can be bubbly and alive even when things in their life are seemingly falling apart. Take a person who is terminally ill, yet whose spirit is more vibrant than another who is in perfect health. And vice-versa. A person who has everything—wealth, health, power, prestige and status—yet is the most miserable person on the face of the earth. And he or she is quick to tell you so! Can this dramatic difference in outlook, in attitude, be explained by saying that some people live by a higher standard, that they are aware of a greater truth that others are not aware of? To come back to our earlier cartoon, do they KNOW something we don't know?

To answer this question, I created a term that I call the **HRR factor.** It addresses the key elements that define our ability to keep "on purpose," to keep focused and moving ahead. It's a sort of "drive-ability" quotient or "unstopability" index.

The HRR factor is made up of three elements:

H—*happiness.* Being positive and enthusiastic, despite what the world is telling us.

    R—*resiliency.* Being able to cope, indeed, overcome ANY obstacle or adversity, and still move ahead.

        R—*resourcefulness.* Being able to find the insight and energy to seize opportunities in order to achieve the results that are important to us.

So let's ask:

The tendency
of man's nature to good
is like the tendency of water
to flow downwards.

MENCIUS
CHINESE PHILOSOPHER AND TEACHER
(371-288 B.C.)

1. Who is happy, as a matter of choice? 2. Who is resilient, best equipped to overcome adversity? and 3. Who is resourceful, able to be creative and take purposeful action in pursuit of cherished goals? From what we have learned, we now have sufficient insight to answer all of these questions.

We know happiness, resiliency and resourcefulness do not depend on age, sex, place of birth, level of education or occupation. It comes, first, from having an internal focus, an internal locus of control—from looking INWARD rather than just outward to find meaning and purpose in our life; and second, once looking inward, from knowing who we really are, our True Self. Remember Lucy admonishing Charlie Brown: "Charlie Brown, you are the one who has to believe. Why don't you ask YOURSELF?"

So it is through our understanding of who we really are that we have the most happiness, the most resiliency, and the most resourcefulness. Various religious teachings give us the most insight into the nature of our True Self. In the Christian faith, for example, it is believed that God chose Jesus Christ as His instrument to teach us about Him and what kind of life we should live. In the Bible, Jesus says, "I am the way, the truth, and the life. . . . "

Man's greatest dilemma is, and always has been, a moral dilemma: to do good or not to do good; to love or not to love; to show compassion or not to show compassion; to forgive or not to forgive; to contribute or not to contribute. The focus necessarily falls on our moral values—what we decide to believe as individuals regarding what is right or wrong, good or bad, fair or unfair, honest or dishonest. We each must decide whose rules we are going to follow and what standards we are going to live by.

Prince Charles of England, in a speech at the College of William and Mary in Williamsburg, Virginia on February 13, 1993, asked the following question: "Why is it that while the means for achieving happiness have never been greater, the incidence of stress and depression also seems to be greater than ever before?"

I believe the answer lies in this fact: **people's expectations have risen without a corresponding increase in personal responsibility.**

The ideas I stand
for are not mine.
I borrowed them
from Socrates. I swiped
them from Chesterfield.
I stole them from Jesus.
And I put them in a book.
If you don't like their rules,
whose would you use?

DALE CARNEGIE
AUTHOR OF *HOW TO WIN FRIENDS*
AND INFLUENCE PEOPLE
(1888-1955)

Some people blame, at least in part, government and its many social assistance programs, including welfare and unemployment insurance. With some families being third, and even fourth generation welfare recipients, they ask the question, "Through these programs, is government stifling or stimulating individual effort and initiative? Is it hindering or helping people to accept 100 percent responsibility for every aspect of their life?" But clearly big government does not deserve all the blame.

The Global Scorecard Says . . .

The global scorecard says that crime is rampant and growing everywhere in the world. And it's not just limited to poor and underdeveloped countries where illiteracy, starvation and poverty are a way of life. In fact, it seems that the explosion in crime and moral decay is largely taking place in developed countries where literacy, abundance and wealth are more common. The United States is generally considered to be the most prosperous, free and capitalistic country in the world. Yet all of our jails are busting at the seams. New jails can't be built fast enough to accommodate all the new arrivals. Authorities are having to push people prematurely out the back door to allow others in the front. **Today, every 22 minutes, someone is murdered in the United States.** The question has to be asked: why is all this moral decay and disrespect for law and order so prevalent where there is so much to be had? And what are some possible solutions to the problem that have some chance of working?

One of the largest industrial activities on earth centers around an armaments industry whose main objective is to protect us from one another. Clearly our greatest enemy is ourselves! Our greatest preoccupation is safety: keeping us from each others' throats. Most of the headlines in today's newspapers focus on one group or another somewhere in the world that is intent on beating up on its neighbor—and on occasion, even trying to annihilate him, to wipe him off the face of the earth.

*To laugh often and much;
to win the respect of intelligent
people and the affection of
children; to earn the appreciation
of honest critics and endure the
betrayal of false friends;
to appreciate beauty;
to find the best in others;
to leave the world a bit better,
whether by a happy child,
a garden patch or a
redeemed social condition;
to know even one life has
breathed easier
because you have lived.
This is to have succeeded.*

RALPH WALDO EMERSON
AMERICAN ESSAYIST,
PHILOSOPHER AND POET
(1803-1882)

Conflict as a Primeval Inheritance

Sadly, there is nothing new in all of this. Ethnic hatred and communal violence from time immemorial have turned man against man, tribe against tribe, nation against nation. Anthropologist Robert Harding of the University of Pennsylvania, an expert on apes and monkeys who live in the wild, believes man is acting not unlike his prehistoric cousins in this regard. He states, "There are virtually no primates that live in a condition where each group has regular, peaceful relationships with other groups. There is usually some form of conflict." Conflicts can be over food resources, territory or sexual partners. It seems these animals form small groups with which they then identify for their safety and survival. Harvard psychiatrist Dr. John Mack believes the Los Angeles riots in 1991 demonstrate a typical example of the survival group. He states, "The gang was the primary identification of (these kids) because they found nothing in the city or the nation with which to identify."

He goes on. "The psychological functions served by that identification are common to all conflicts: survival, a sense of self-worth. These are all fundamental psychological principles, a sense of having power versus powerlessness. When threatened, the group we identify with for our survival, whether it be on a family, ethnic or national level, defines our sense of self."

Mack continues. "Any political thinker who seeks a fellowship of all mankind . . . must recognize the psychological meaning of the identity of self with the nation. Failure to do so will limit such concepts as brotherhood of man to philosophical and utopian visions and imaginings."

The solution to man's dilemma seems clear. Consider the effect if the great masses of humanity were to identify, on an individual basis, with a higher power, a God whose very embodiment is love and compassion and justice. In such an instance, the focus moves away from individuals, groups and nations having to band together for security to mankind joyfully joining hands together as a species for the betterment of all.

The only difference,
the very only one, between those
who are free and the others,
is that those who are free have begun
to understand what they really are
and have begun to practice it.

RICHARD BACH
FROM *JONATHAN LIVINGSTON SEAGULL*

If we all saw each other—regardless of race, color, creed, nationality or religion—as part of the family of God, all as one's brother or one's sister, much of what is wrong with the world today would melt away.

The Eternal Search for Truth

Who am I? Why am I here? Where am I going? Can I influence this process? These are but some of the questions that have forever haunted the inquisitive mind of man. Man seeks to know himself, and through himself, to know his Maker. Clearly man has not found the answer by harnessing nature's elements and powers, or by building great empires or creating vast wealth. The physical world in which we live is but a temporary thing, forever changing and evolving. It is an effect, not a cause; it is an illusion, not truth.

You may wonder at the slow pace of human evolution. Why are we still so ignorant about so many things? Why can't we seem to get along with each other? Why does envy, distrust and hatred still abound in relationships between individuals, groups and nation states? Richard Carrington puts it all in perspective with this interesting explanation:

"Let us imagine that, by some magic, the whole earth's history could be compressed into a single year. On this scale, the first eight months would be completely without life. The following two would be devoted to the most primitive of creatures. No mammals would appear until the second week in December. Man, as we know him, would strut onto the stage at approximately 11:45 p.m. on December 31. **The age of written history would occupy little more than the last 60 seconds on the clock!**"

From this we see that man has only begun to think! And we need a lot more time if we are to rise above the primeval instincts of our ancestors, if we are to get things right. We must move beyond a preoccupation with safety and security needs to self-actualization as individuals and a species. But how much time do we have—as individuals? As a species? Buckminster Fuller once made this comment: "We are not going to be able to operate our Spaceship Earth successfully nor for much longer unless we see it as a whole spaceship and our fate as common. It has to be everybody or nobody."

The currents of the Universal Being circulate through me; I am part and parcel of God.

RALPH WALDO EMERSON
AMERICAN ESSAYIST,
PHILOSOPHER AND POET
(1803-1882)

We have already shown that thought is first cause. We think. We believe. We imagine. We become. We do. This is how thought is transformed into things. Nothing is done by man alone. All things are done by Universal Mind in response to thought and conviction. What we think returns to us in physical form, good from good and evil from evil. As Lao-Tze has pointed out, "These two things, the spiritual and the material, though we call them by different names, in their origin are one and the same."

In this way, we work through an intelligence that guides and controls the universe. We live in this intelligence. We are a part of it and have access to all of it. We are as small as our earthly existence and as great as our spiritual desires. This intelligence is ours to use as we choose. It is a gift, a divine birthright from God. Through it we can glimpse the limitless dimensions of our true spiritual being, and see that all things are possible. By attunement with Universal Mind, we can gradually free ourselves from the limitations of our personal ego, and allow a greater self to evolve, prosper and grow. For it is only when we are aligned with this spirit that we can hope to manifest the convictions of our heart to discover who we really are.

"To live so as to keep human consciousness in constant relation with the divine, the spiritual and the eternal, is to individualize infinite power."—Mary Baker Eddy

Human life is the medium through which Universal Mind seeks to show itself, and each of us plays our part to this end. When we have completed our tasks and made our contributions here on earth, it is time for us to leave and return from whence we came. At death, we all become one with Universal Mind.

From all that we have learned, from the spiritual awakening that we have experienced, we come to realize the greatest truth of all: since God dwells within Universal Mind and Universal Mind dwells in each of us . . .

*One word frees us
of all weight and pain of life:
that word is love.*

SOPHOCLES
GREEK TRAGIC DRAMATIST
(496-406 B.C.)

He is our True Self!

At last, our journey is complete. **We now know who we really are! We have finally discovered the ULTIMATE INSIGHT.**

Conclusion

It all comes down to this. We think. But we don't create the thoughts. We just have them. We believe. We imagine. We become. We do. And as we believe and imagine and become and do, these same things are manifested in our life. But not by us. They are manifested by the same spirit that created the thoughts in the first place. So whatever we think and believe, whether good or bad, right or wrong, just or unjust, is manifested in our life by a power other than ourselves, yet unquestionably greater than ourselves. Knowing this is our great freedom, our great salvation. For we need only focus our beliefs and thoughts on what is good and on what is right. And having done this, these very things will be manifested in our physical world by divine action. We don't have to fret; we don't have to force; we don't have to fight. We need only choose the right thoughts that are consistent with the world we want to help create. Faith in a higher power does all the rest.

If we change our dominant thoughts, if we change our focus according to what we think is right and just and good, we will change the world! It all starts with one individual, who influences and changes another individual, who influences and changes another individual . . . the power of one in action!

What about you? Do you want to be an active participant in this magnificent journey? Or do you want to be a lonely spectator watching from a distance? If your answer to the second question is yes, then begin with this simple first step: SEE ONLY LOVE IN *ALL THINGS*—in the good, the bad and the ugly you come into contact with every day. It is surely there. Love has the greatest power to do good in the world. You need only acknowledge it to have it manifested in your life.

Herein lies one of the great paradoxes in life. It can be argued that we can't give love away until we have it, and that we can't have it until we give it away. In truth, when we have developed the ability

*You will find as
you look back upon your life
that the moments when you
have really lived, are
the moments when you have
done things in a
spirit of love.*

HENRY DRUMMOND
SCOTTISH CLERGYMAN AND WRITER
(1851-1897)

to give love away, emotionally and spiritually—and unconditionally—and then do this in practice, we find we have it in our life. It comes by giving it away.

Isn't it interesting—almost everything we know in our lives at one time or another goes out of style. Think about it. Cars, homes, clothes, movies, TV programs, certain expressions, jewelry, cosmetics, wall paper, books, computer software, colors, glassware, watches, various foods, skyscrapers, light fixtures and furniture. The list is endless. And these are the everyday things most of us build our lives around. But what is the one thing that has NEVER gone out of style, that is timeless, enduring, that has been with us since man first appeared on this planet? Of course. It is love.

To conclude with some of our key findings, remember that

> 1. Life is a series of thoughts.
> 2. We become what we think about.
> 3. We can choose what we think about.

These are the primary connecting links in the Personal Empowerment Process. We empower ourselves by gaining control over our thoughts and actions in order to get the results we want, the emotional and material rewards we all so desperately seek in life.

Our greatest responsibility, then, is simply to act as we know we should. Knowing this, Saint Paul offers the following sage advice in Philippians 4:8,9 about what to think about and focus on:

> Finally, brethren, whatever things are true, whatever things are noble, whatever things are just, whatever things are pure, whatever things are lovely, whatever things are of good report, if there is any virtue and if there is anything praiseworthy—meditate on these things . . . and the God of peace will be with you.

*I believe that love will finally
establish the Kingdom of God on earth,
and that the cornerstones
of that Kingdom will be
Liberty, Truth, Brotherhood and Service.*

HELEN KELLER
AMERICAN WRITER AND LECTURER
(1880-1968)

YOU HAVE TO SET YOURSELF ON F-I-R-E!

MOTHER TERESA

Mother Teresa was born Agnes Gonxha Bojaxhiu on August 27, 1910 in Skopje, Albania. As a young girl, she heard about the Bengali missions in India through newsletters written by Yugoslavian Jesuit priests serving there. Agnes soon developed a great interest in the work of the Christian missions in India that were dedicated to spreading Christianity and the word of God among Hindu society. The rigid caste system in place there provided a unique opportunity for conversion of the masses to Christianity, thereby allowing them to live a life of dignity and self-respect. She joined the Order of Our Lady of Loreto based in Ireland, and traveled to Entally in Calcutta to teach at a high school run by Loreto sisters. She taught there for almost 20 years.

In 1946, Mother Teresa received a new calling from God to leave her relatively secure position at the school to serve the poorest of the poor in the Indian cities. While educating the children of the relatively well-to-do middle class, she couldn't help but be moved by the desperate plight and appalling conditions of thousands of people living in the streets who lacked food, water, clothing and basic health care.

In 1950, with the Pope's permission, she went on to form her own order of nuns known as the Missionaries of Charity. Today it has over 340 centers in more than 50 countries around the world. There are well over 2,000 sisters and brothers in the Missionaries of Charity, with almost 50,000 lay co-workers active world-wide in the cause. All have joined Mother Teresa in committing their lives to Jesus Christ—to sharing, giving love, and doing God's work. In 1979, the world recognized Mother Teresa and her contribution to mankind by awarding her the Nobel Peace prize.

You make a difference by giving something of yourself for the betterment of others. Mother Teresa has made a difference. She dared to dream big dreams, and in the process, she set herself on fire!

But if a man happens to find himself, he has a mansion which he can inhabit with dignity all the days of his life.

JAMES MICHENER
AMERICAN NOVELIST

*God created each of us
in His own image.
He put a little of Himself
—His love, His grace, His power—
in each of us.
Unfortunately, this is
the last place
most of us think to look
to find it.*

WALTER STAPLES